Half A Brain:

Confessions of a Special Needs Mom

Jenni Basch

Copyright @2020 by Jenni Basch

First printing 2020

ISBN 978-1-7346786-0-4

Book cover design by ebooklaunch.com
Formatting by Polgarus Studio

Published by Mile 18 Press

Author website: jennibasch.com

To my chubby pigs

Chapter One

When I was younger, I had no desire to have children. I would break out in emotional hives just thinking about having my own child. My friend Amy wanted five children, and I think the only thing stopping her at that point was the fact that we were fourteen and she didn't have a boyfriend. She was wistful. I felt disgust.

Years later, I stood on the front porch of our rented house in California, heavily pregnant, when the phone rang. I leaned against the railing and examined the floorboard. The porch was the best part of the house, with its old-timey boards and slanted, covered roof. Some of the nails on the floorboard stuck up a bit, so my husband would hammer them down only to have different ones pop up the next week, whack-a-mole style.

"They found a mass on your baby's brain," my midwife said.

I held my belly tightly and sucked in my breath.

"How big?" I asked.

"Very," she said.

She didn't know anything else. I hung up the phone and held it loosely in my hand. I looked up at my neighbor's house and watched as she meticulously watered her plants. Another neighbor threw a ball with his young son in their yard. I didn't understand why they were smiling. Didn't they see the world crumbling beneath them?

I looked down at my huge belly and cringed. I imagined I carried a monster with sharp talons, slimy scales, and contorted facial features. She would be born a freak. I knew my life would forever be altered because of this mass. No matter the outcome, my life would become harder.

When I told my husband, Adam, what the midwife said about the mass, he said we didn't know anything yet, and we needed more information. I listened to what he said, but I felt the baby kick. I was seriously about to freak out. I had a baby girl inside me, kicking and punching, and she had a mass - on her brain. I cried because it's all I could think to do. The tears flowed.

I called my friend who lived three thousand miles away in Wisconsin. She answered. Through sobs, I said, "I don't think my baby is going to make it."

"Jenni," she said, "slow down and tell me what's going on."

I told her that the pregnancy had seemed fine. I had gone that morning for an ultrasound to rule out my baby being breech. I was suspicious because the ultrasound exam took longer than usual. The sonographer called in her supervisor who looked at the scanned images and asked when I would next meet with my midwife.

Next week, I told them, and they exchanged subtle glances. Their body language gave them away. The supervisor smiled and wished me well with the birth, indicating the end of the appointment. I wasn't sure what was going on but I felt a sense of calm wrapped in heavy denial. I walked out of the office and went home, not mentioning my moment of suspicion and fear to my husband.

I didn't tell Adam about the appointment because I thought I had dodged a bullet. It didn't seem possible that anything horrible could happen to me. I knew everything would be fine and I could return to my life in a bubble of ease and comfort.

My friend and I talked for a bit longer and I told her I would fill her in once I knew more. I paced the house. After a few hours, my midwife called again and said that the diagnostic center wanted me to come in for a more comprehensive ultrasound scheduled for the next day. I spent some time online but it proved inconclusive. The exact nature of the mass remained a mystery.

After I went in for the comprehensive ultrasound, Adam and I waited in a separate room while the doctor and sonographer looked at the scans. When they came into the room, I hoped for some clarity. I desperately wanted the mass to be something insignificant, like a smudge on the screen.

"What is it?" we asked.

"We aren't sure," the doctor said, "because although this is the best machine we have in our area, it's not showing us enough detail. But we think she might have Dandy Walker Syndrome. Might be something else. Either way, it looks grim."

I remember him using the word "grim" because it sounded like a word Stephen King uses in his stories. I imagined one of King's characters, dying in a pile of blood and entrails, saying, "boy, the chances of me saving the world seem grim."

The doctor said that when I had my next child, it would probably go better for me. He sounded like the world's biggest asshole. Did he forget about the baby presently living in my uterus? I looked at the female sonographer, begging her with my eyes to think about this baby, but she nodded her head in agreement that the next baby would be better. The sonographer suggested we get an even more advanced ultrasound in either L.A. or San Francisco. We chose L.A. because Adam's aunt and uncle lived there.

The doctor said that his secretary would arrange an

"How long until the appointment?" Adam asked

"Probably in a week or so, depending on the h schedule," the doctor said.

A week or so sounded like an eternity to have a dying baby writhing around inside of me, but we told them to start the process since they didn't have anything else to offer.

I sat in shock. I noticed the doctor's sterile gloves and wondered why he had them on during a consult. A large machine sat in the corner, emitting a slow and steady beeping sound. I thought for a moment that I may have left the stove burner on and our house could be filled with poisonous gas. Then I came back into myself. We were knee deep in crap.

Chapter Two

I looked up Dandy Walker Syndrome as soon as I walked into the house. The doctor was correct about it being a "grim" prognosis. Dandy Walker Syndrome is a brain malformation that affects cognitive and physical development. The prognosis varies, but it would certainly result in a lifetime of delays and problems. I spent the next twenty-four hours looking at articles, case studies, and diagrams. I cried continuously the whole time because it seemed terrible and awful and hopeless.

Adam tried to get me to stop looking but I told him to buzz off. He remained sympathetic throughout the entire process and tried to be supportive, but I felt like he didn't understand at all. He seemed almost unaffected by the news and somehow continued to live his life exactly as he had before.

He didn't research or discuss the information I had found. I felt like it was all up to me. I felt incredulous. If our unborn daughter did have Dandy Walker Syndrome, at least one of us was actually doing something about it. But I didn't complain. I felt like he blamed me for being pregnant in the first place, bringing pain which we shouldn't have had to endure.

Adam and I entered our marriage (July of 2005, for those keeping track) with the understanding that we would not have children. For the first few years of our marriage, we both worked as high school teachers in Ohio. I grew dissatisfied with the teaching profession and decided to pursue a long time love of mine - counseling. I wanted to do therapy in private practice, or work with teenagers in a school setting. I studied psychology as an undergraduate and I had always wanted to pursue it further.

I also began to detest the Midwestern gray skies, which take up nearly half of each calendar year. By October, Ohioans place their sunglasses, dresses, sandals, bathing suits, and shorts into a box that does not get looked at for the next six months. Mid-April, the box comes out and is emptied, usually with glee. Then all the sweaters, corduroys, boots, coats, gloves, scarves, and winter hats are placed in the box and stored in a closet for the next six months.

These reasons began to weigh on me and I began to plan a move to somewhere more exotic. Adam liked the idea of moving, so I applied to graduate schools on the West Coast. After I received my acceptance letters and visited most of the campuses, we gave notice to our respective employers and moved to the central coast of California in the summer of 2007. I attended Cal Poly where I eventually earned an MS in counseling psychology.

After a few months of attending graduate school, I felt a powerful shift in my psyche. For the first time in my life, my body ached when I saw a pregnant woman, a swaddled baby, or a mother and her son holding hands while crossing the street. I had dreams of holding a baby boy and had visual hallucinations of babies swirling around my head. Babies were so foreign to my mind that I had a hard time understanding what was happening. I felt a ticking sensation in my loins and a tortuous yearning. I turned into a cliché.

At thirty-one years old, I finally understood why some of my friends held such strong convictions about motherhood. Even some of my hopelessly single friends would gush about the day they would have their own baby to hold and snuggle, planning their IVF dates in case they didn't find a suitable partner soon enough. I used to think they were crazy or that maybe I was missing some sort of maternal chip in my brain. But suddenly, I couldn't stop thinking about babies!

At first, I avoided telling Adam that I had suddenly become a different person. Who was I to suddenly change my mind when we had mutually agreed a few years earlier? But I simply felt like I was going mad with the idea of having children, and I had to broach the subject with him.

When I approached him with the idea, he was surprised but not shocked. Adam is perhaps the most easy-going person I know, so we talked about it without judgment or tears or anger. He didn't jump in head first, but he wasn't completely opposed either. It went as well as I could have hoped, and we decided to let the idea percolate for a few months so we could make a sound decision.

My desire to have a baby only became stronger, and even though I had started graduate school, I felt like waiting to finish the program first would be a bad idea due to my age. I worried we might not become pregnant quickly or we might want more than one child. Although I knew plenty of women who gave birth in their late thirties and early forties, I didn't want that for myself.

I've always feared the inevitability of my own early death at age fifty-five because that is the age at which my mother died. When I started calculating, I panicked thinking of giving birth even one day later than necessary. My brother was still in high school when my mother died and his educational future was deeply affected by her death. Therefore, I felt determined to have grown children by that arbitrary age.

After a few months of growing certainty that I should have children, and multiple candid discussions with Adam, we decided to have a baby. We opened it up to the universe and I became pregnant the very next month. Once I read the positive pregnancy test, I took a deep breath. A rush of emotions hit me. I didn't know what to think or how to feel. I knew the baby was a boy, although we didn't officially find out until months later. Score one for mama's intuition.

I had a fairly easy pregnancy, although I gained too much weight. I continued attending graduate classes, but planned to take a quarter off after the birth. I planned a natural birth, but my son was a surprise breech and I ended up with a C-section.

Deeply disappointed to have a C-section and frustrated with how the situation had been handled by my midwife, I vowed to have an ultrasound done at the end of any subsequent pregnancies. In that case, I would know if the baby was breech and could try to turn the position of the baby, avoiding another C-section.

My infant son liked to cuddle and never wanted to leave anyone's arms. He rarely napped and woke upon a slight sound or movement. He breastfed for long periods of time and demanded precision. I felt more passion and fatigue than I ever thought possible. I learned that I could actually love someone so much that I would jump in front of a train for them.

Shortly after my son turned one, we decided to have another baby. I wanted a daughter, especially in light of the fact that my own mother had died. I knew I couldn't replace my mother, but I craved the mother-daughter relationship with its intimate interactions and conversations.

I missed talking to my mom on the phone when I felt proud or scared or angry or joyful. After my son's birth, I yearned to ask her when my teeth fell out and what size shoe I wore in first grade. I wanted to know what she felt like when she married my father and if she had heartburn during her pregnancies. I wanted to ask her about the aging process.

I knew I couldn't order up a baby girl like a cheeseburger, but I figured it couldn't hurt to think about my intention of having one. We planned to wait a few months so I could have the baby after graduation, but instead I got pregnant right away. I spoke with my professors and made some preliminary plans for a possible early graduation date.

Helpful Hint: If you ever find yourself pregnant during graduate school, finish early! Juggling a breastfeeding baby in one hand and a textbook extolling the wonders of rhetorical discourse in the other is not fun!

The pregnancy felt easier than my first, and I suffered no complications. I gained less weight, and I knew what to expect during each trimester. Despite pregnancy fatigue, graduate school stress, and raising a one-year old, I somehow managed.

I switched to a new midwife who I trusted from the moment we met in her office. During my twenty-week ultrasound, we learned the gender of our baby. It was a girl! I couldn't believe my luck. I loved thinking about her precious cheeks and fingers and toes developing inside my womb. Our midwife also scheduled an ultrasound for my thirty-sixth week of pregnancy to rule out another breech scenario.

This thirty-six week ultrasound scan resulted in the phone call telling me about the mass on my daughter's brain. The days after the call were somber and tense. I could not function on anything but autopilot. Daily activities seemed cumbersome and joyless.

The diagnostic center hadn't called with an appointment yet and I grew restless. A family friend who was a doctor read the ultrasound scans and painted me a pretty ugly picture. She recommended not resuscitating my daughter if given the opportunity after birth.

I felt like she had stabbed me in the chest, twisted the knife around, and sliced open my heart. I buckled over and stifled a scream.

But I pushed myself back to standing and listened. I needed to hear the truth. She gave me sound advice and recommended going to an appropriate emergency room if I felt anything suspicious with the baby. She said that our local hospital wouldn't staff the neurosurgeons necessary to perform life-saving surgery, so we would need to travel to a larger city.

Since we became more restless and hopeless every moment, Adam and I decided to drive the four hours south and crash the ER at an L.A. hospital. We went to Cedars-Sinai Medical Center because our midwife found great reviews about their Neonatal Intensive Care Unit (NICU). Due to its Beverly Hills location, many celebrities gave birth there, so I figured it must be great. We quickly packed a bag, called Adam's parents, and drove south.

Chapter Three

When we arrived, I told the ER attendants there was something wrong with the baby and I was scared she would die.

Fun Fact: When a large, waddling pregnant woman tells ER staff that her baby is dying, she skips the line and gets seen before the guy with a purple growth on his neck.

After processing our insurance and signing forms that assured the hospital we would pay for any services rendered, an attendant pushed me in a wheelchair to a room on the emergency floor. Nurses placed leads and IVs while doctors asked a million questions. Adam and I gave as much concise, detailed information as possible.

During that situation, and during subsequent ER visits, ambulance rides, near-death experiences, and the chronic cacophony of my daughter's random neurological events, I functioned like a cyborg. My brain doled out logical responses and completely shut off my emotions. I had honed the skill over decades of practice. Although it served me well in these critical times, it has also made me appear too serious or cold at times.

In the hospital room, various medical people talked about my unborn daughter in such clinical, pessimistic ways that I had to compartmentalize my feelings and deal with them later. Cedars-Sinai is a teaching hospital, so it had numerous residents, interns, and nursing students who "really should come in here and see this ultrasound," because it isn't every day that such a gruesome situation is presented in live, observable form.

I endured countless ultrasounds and MRIs. Multiple specialists, surgeons, obstetricians, and oncologists visited and attempted to reach a consensus. This was indeed a "grim" proposition. Every doctor said it was really, really bad, but they couldn't reach an agreement about what the brain mass might be and how to proceed.

The debate settled into two main camps. The surgeons wanted the baby out so they could cut into her head and figure out if the mass was a brain tumor, a hemorrhage, or some sort of malformation. The obstetricians wanted her to stay inside me until at least thirty-seven weeks in order to maximize lung function and chance of survival outside the womb.

Even with all the dire, grim, terrible news I heard, I still held onto a sliver of hope. Every time someone said my daughter would probably die within thirty minutes of being born, that miniscule hope helped me plod along.

I knew that if she died in the hospital surgical ward, I couldn't leave her in L.A. I talked with my cousin who works as a funeral director. He knew how to move a body up to the central coast and arrange an appropriate burial. I enlisted his help and told him to wait on standby. It may sound horrific to think about a funeral, but I wanted a service to have some sort of closure for my daughter. I needed the ritual.

For the next few days, doctors debated, discussed, furrowed their brows, and consulted articles and retired colleagues. One doctor consulted a renowned former colleague of his in Israel. Eventually the obstetricians won the proverbial "argument" and we were discharged to give the baby more time to develop and optimize her chance of survival. We drove home and waited.

We existed in an even more tense and depressing sense of limbo. We had spent days listening to smart doctors tell us that our daughter would die shortly after birth and there wasn't anything we could do about it. Home felt stale and uneasy. We couldn't relax with the constant reminders of the impending birth. In addition to my swollen belly, our house contained a new dresser, co-sleeper, infant diapers, girl onesies, pants, shirts, bibs, pink socks, and an embroidered blanket with our daughter's name: Skye.

The next morning, our hospital-based social worker called and asked me a question: When we returned for the birth, did I want a photograph of my dead baby taken by a professional photographer? She said this with the utmost sincerity. It was a legitimate question and I said that, yes, I did want a photograph. Even though the moment would be excruciating, I felt that photographic evidence of her would be special in the long run.

The process of planning for horrific days to come reminded me of going with my mother to the funeral home and making arrangements for her imminent death. About six months before her death of lung cancer, she and I went to the funeral home and looked at pictures of urns, caskets, headstones, and burial plots. We scanned the menu options like we were choosing a dinner entree. I imagined speaking with a thick British accent: "Yes, that urn looks delightful; I'll take one of those with a cremation on the side."

One of the biggest regrets of my life happened as a result of this visit to the funeral home. When the funeral director said we needed to have an outfit for her burial, my mother brightened and said she wanted to buy a pink suit, like the one that Jackie Kennedy wore on the day of her husband's murder in the Dallas motorcade. She even had a magazine with women modeling different versions of such suits. I have no idea why I even said anything, but when she looked at me and asked what I thought, I mentioned a plain blue skirt and white shirt she already owned as seeming "more genuinely her."

"Why spend the money unnecessarily," I said to her.

My mother used to be quite fashionable in her twenties and thirties, and she bought interesting, quality brands. After having children and spending less money on herself, she bought clothing from the thrift store, if at all. She was also notoriously cheap, so that small comment from me was all it took to change her mind.

I wish she had said "screw you" to me and bought the damn pink suit anyway. Instead she never mentioned it again and we buried her in an old blue skirt and a shapeless, white shirt. Although I know her body has decomposed and the clothes now hang off her in shreds, I am ashamed that I didn't tell her to buy whatever she wanted.

She deserved that small token and so much more. It had nothing to do with me or anyone else. She wanted to reclaim a small part of her true self and I helped stifle that. I will never forgive myself.

Chapter Four

Shortly after the social worker called and asked us about obtaining post-birth photographs, Adam's phone rang. A hospital admitting representative said that the doctors wanted to do a C-section the next morning at 10:30, and we needed to be there at 8:00. The doctors had met and agreed that the next day would be acceptable to everyone because I would be exactly thirty-seven weeks pregnant.

Adam and I looked at each other, wide-eyed, and started packing and preparing our son to leave again. We had been home for less than twenty-four hours. I had mixed feelings, but I truly wanted the baby out of my belly. For better or worse, I needed to face my destiny and birth this baby. I knew that I had to deal with the hell I was about to endure.

I called a friend and asked her to be on standby for removing all aspects of my daughter from our home. If Skye died, my friend would take out the dresser, infant girl clothes, and co-sleeper. I didn't care where it went. I told her that I couldn't look at any of it ever again.

Luckily my mother-in-law flew in from Ohio that night in order to watch my son and allow Adam and I the luxury of focusing on the birth. I sincerely appreciate all that his family did for us. We would have managed with our son there as witness to our daughter's birth, but Rowan (who wasn't even two yet) would fare much better with his grandmother than with the spectacle that awaited us.

With Rowan settled in with his grandmother and great-aunt in L.A., Adam and I reported to Cedars Sinai in the morning, giving our insurance information again and waiting to be taken upstairs to a pre-surgical bed. I felt calm but anxious, stoic but scared. Dread weighed down my body like lead. I paced and stood and paced some more.

> **Helpful Hint:** If you find yourself in a hospital admitting area, be prepared to wait anywhere from twenty seconds to six hours.

Eventually a hospital employee led us to the pre-surgical ward. We had to wait for the actual C-section due to a small procedural matter. I had eaten a few bites of sandwich later than I should have, which I fessed up to in case it became lodged in my windpipe and asphyxiated me during surgery.

The few extra hours worked in our favor because our midwife arrived during that time. She drove down to L.A. to see us, and her generosity and words of wisdom gave me great solace. Being in the birthing business gave her insight and experience into every possible scenario. She reassured us that we would get through this day and there would be good days to come.

During the wait, I had an intense longing to visit the hospital chapel. Even though my "devout Catholic" membership card had long since expired, I ventured downstairs and entered the chapel door. I looked around for kneelers, but since Cedars Sinai is a Jewish hospital, I found only yarmulkes. Instead, I knelt down on the altar, huge belly and all, and I clasped my hands together in prayer. Since I was alone, I spoke aloud and with great passion.

I prayed to my mother, to the Virgin Mary, to any gods or goddesses listening. I prayed to my ancestors and anyone else who had gone through anything similar that might help me in this time. I prayed for my daughter to live. I prayed for the strength to get through whatever might happen in a few hours. I honestly had no idea how I would get through delivering a dead baby. I could feel her kicking me while I spoke, making the prospect even more painful.

How could a baby who was kicking and moving be dead in two hours? How would I bury my daughter? How would I get through that moment? Since I had undergone a C-section before, I felt terrified about lying on my back, helpless, when she came out dead. How long would they let me see her? Would they sew me back up so I could actually sit up and hold her? Would I be stuck lying down on the operating table, cradling my dead baby on my side, staring at her vacant eyes? Would twenty people on the operating team watch it happen? Is that how I would meet my daughter?

When I prayed for my daughter's life, I told anyone listening to me that I could handle anything. I pleaded and begged like a man with a noose around his neck.

Once I returned to the pre-surgical room, we waited for a few more hours until the nurses and doctors began entering in more rapid succession. Interns, residents, nursing students, fellows, nurse practitioners, obstetricians, surgeons, anesthesiologists, and charge nurses entered the room in intervals. They checked my IV, took my vitals (temperature, blood pressure, and pulse), fixed a malfunctioning lead, verified allergies, discussed risks and possible scenarios, and vaguely guessed at when someone would take me to the prep room.

Suddenly a dapper man in scrubs entered the room and introduced himself as Dr. Moise Danielpour, Head of Pediatric Neurosurgery. He walked with an air of importance and intelligence. The nurses and attendees in the room stood up and stopped what they were doing.

He looked at my chart for a moment, then looked at me, and said, "I can help your baby." I stopped breathing for a moment. I thought I must be hallucinating. I looked him squarely in the eye and saw only sincerity.

"If she cries when she comes out, she has a chance. This isn't a death sentence." He pointed to her chart. "But if she isn't crying and is ashen in color, survival isn't viable."

Who was this handsome prince of mine, coming out of seemingly nowhere? He was the first person who gave us any glimmer of hope and I clung to it like a drowning swimmer. Dr. Danielpour explained that with his expertise and experience, he would be involved if she lived.

He believed that Skye had a brain hemorrhage, not a tumor or any sort of malformation like Dandy Walker. If she survived the birth and stabilized, he could operate and help alleviate some of the issues. Thinking about an operation didn't faze me at that moment because if he operated, that meant she was alive. I might be able to cancel those funeral arrangements after all.

"It's all about that initial cry," he reiterated. "We will know more as soon as she comes out." After he spoke with us, things moved quickly. I swallowed some anti-nausea goop, had my IVs triple-checked, blood pressure and temperature taken, said goodbye to Adam, and lay down on the gurney taking me to the surgical prep room. All I could think about was the initial few seconds after she came out. I dreaded those seconds.

Chapter Five

The prep room felt clinical and scary. The room contained huge pieces of equipment, industrial sinks, tall cabinets, and various people dressed in scrubs scurrying in and out. A doctor inserted a needle into my spine while I sat shivering.

> **Fun Fact:** Hospital rooms are always freezing cold. I think that's why they have so many blankets. Feel free to ask for as many as you want.

Some of the people in the room introduced themselves and others just adjusted a knob, peered at my spinal incision, or looked at my chart. After ten minutes, the spinal injection had numbed my bottom half sufficiently to take me into the surgical room.

The orderlies wheeled me into the middle of the room while I lay on my back, numb from the waist down, a surgical gown loosely covering me. Both female obstetricians performing the C-section met with me and spoke about the procedure and its possible outcomes. The anesthesiologist sat behind my head with various beeping machines and IVs surrounding him. He would guide the entire procedure, like the captain of a large sailing vessel.

I received my first lesson about the pecking order in a hospital chain. The surgery wouldn't happen without an anesthesiologist.

They make the final decision about surgical worthiness. One nurse told me she regarded anesthesiologists more highly than surgeons, who themselves hold a status close to godliness.

After speaking with the obstetricians, I glanced around the room, aghast. I counted at least twenty-five people in the room. Only three people had assisted when my son was born via C-section. I asked the anesthesiologist to explain. He listed them in clusters, including the NICU staff, emergency responder nurses, students, interns, residents, nurse assistants, nurse practitioners, Dr. Danielpour, and the two obstetricians performing the surgery.

"Is this normal?" I asked.

"Not really." He shrugged. "We just don't know what's going to happen."

Even with all his experience, he just had to get through the day one case at a time.

Adam, dressed in scrubs, entered the room and stood on my left side. I'm sure he felt terrified. Someone placed a large blue curtain over my waist to block the view of the surgical site. I didn't need to watch a human baby thrash her way out of a large open wound in my gut. Seeing my internal organs casually placed on my blood-soaked abdomen wouldn't be a great way to start my birth process either.

The doctors began the procedure, and I lay as still as I could, focusing on the buzz of machines and the conversation between the obstetricians. The anesthesiologist gave me periodic updates on the surgery's progress, and I gave him periodic updates on the subtle tugs and pulls I felt in my abdomen. I had a nasty pain in my right side. When I reported it to him, he pumped up the volume on something and it felt better immediately.

After fifteen minutes, one of the obstetricians peeped her head around the curtain and said, "One minute to birth." Her head disappeared and my heart sank. It was the most excruciating sixty seconds of my life. If I hadn't been slit open like a slaughtered cow, I would have run as far away as possible to avoid the situation.

During that moment, I closed my eyes and took a deep breath. Not speaking aloud, I willed my daughter to hear my thoughts. I told her with all my heart that if she needed to go, I would let her go. I would handle the fallout and the depression and the anger and the sadness. If it was her time, then it was done. But in the same breath, I told her if she was willing to fight, then I was willing to fight too. I promised her that I would fight forever for her. I told her the decision was hers.

In sixty seconds, a person can drive approximately one mile on the highway, wash three or four dishes, or give a presentation in class on the eating habits of the wombat. In sixty seconds, a person can also lament how fleeting life is, how painful life is, and how long sixty seconds itself can seem to last.

All I could think about was that damn cry.

"Come on and cry, please baby girl, please just cry when you come out!"

I felt increasingly desperate. The doctors quickened their pace and I experienced immense pressure in my abdomen, indicating the baby was about to emerge. They pulled her out, excitement and anticipation evident in their breathing, and after an almost endless couple seconds, I heard my baby utter a loud, long cry. She cried!

"What color is she?" I yelled over the cacophony of working professionals and a screaming infant.

It took a moment but someone told me she was pale, but not ashen. While I visually searched the room for her, the obstetricians worked to reposition my organs in my abdomen and sew up the incision. I felt more subtle pulls and tugs, but they barely registered. I felt panic and anger. I wanted to see my baby. I needed to see her face and she needed to see mine.

Finally, a nurse brought her to me. Swaddled in white hospital blankets, she had closed eyes and fat cheeks. The nurse brought Skye's face down to me and I rubbed her cheek with mine, savoring its warmth and smell. Endorphins rushed through my brain and body. Oh, it was so brief! The nurse whisked Skye away and took her to an incubator.

Dr. Danielpour appeared over my head and I cried out to him, "Please save my baby!" Tears erupted from my eyeballs like an exploding dam. He smiled and said he would do his best. He told me that Skye scored a seven on her Apgar, higher than expected.

"I'll see you in the NICU after your recovery," he said, and walked out of the room. While the obstetricians continued sewing up my incision, the NICU staff rolled Skye's incubator out the door. Tears rolling down my face, I watched the incubator as long as I could. Once they left, I focused on getting through the remainder of the procedure.

I felt frustrated that Adam couldn't go with Skye to the NICU, but the doctors said she needed to stabilize first. They asked us about intubation and other lifesaving procedures. It felt like an intrusion. I didn't get a moment to enjoy my daughter's birth, to revel in her survival, to process the myriad emotions flooding my mind and body.

Adam and I said we would decide when and if the time came. It was too difficult to ascertain the what-ifs. We were both shocked that she survived. It seemed cruel and unusual to think about ending her life at that point. It seemed unthinkable.

Chapter Six

After the surgeons sewed me back up, orderlies moved me to an inpatient room where I would spend the next four days recovering. A nurse tucked me into bed, served me a fabulous mix of juice cocktail and ice, and turned off the lights. I asked her when I could go see Skye and she told me I had to be able to stand up and walk at least ten steps without vomiting.

"Usually about twenty-four hours. The spinal has to wear off," she said. "Can't have NICU nurses taking care of the mothers, too."

I wouldn't be able to see my baby for twenty-four hours? Devastation hit me, but I tried to respond.

"I'll do it quicker than that," I said.

I tried to lift my head, and a wave of pain and nausea hit me stone cold. I quickly laid my head back down. The nurse smirked and left the room. I looked at Adam and told him to go see Skye as soon as he could. Obviously, I needed time to recover before I could walk ten steps. For the second time, I would be separated from my new baby.

After having a C-section during my son's birth, I felt sad and longed for a more traditional labor. It probably sounds crazy that I would want to experience the excruciating, majestic pain that must be labor. Having a C-section doesn't make a woman any less of a mother. Having a C-section is bad-ass. It's the ultimate sacrifice. I wouldn't go under the knife to save some random dirtbag on the street.

During the C-section for the birth of my son two years earlier, the ubiquitous blue curtain kept me from seeing him yanked into the world by his feet and butt. I saw him for a brief moment as he screamed in the doctor's arms and then he was weighed, washed, and taken away while orderlies wheeled me downstairs.

That time, I stayed in a basement recovery room for three hours. Meanwhile, Adam sat in our hospital room holding our newly born son skin-to-skin. During those three hours, even though I knew I had a son somewhere in the universe, I felt disconnected. Strangely, I didn't care that he wasn't with me.

I felt more concerned with how to pass the time. A large, orange curtain surrounded my bed. I had a catheter, an IV in the top of my right hand, and a disturbing sense of pressure and pulsating pain in my abdomen.

Instead of experiencing a magical moment with my son after his birth, I lay alone and isolated from my baby. Curtains separated me from a few other women who had also just given birth. I could hear light moans and groans from other women lying in their own orange recovery cocoons.

I too moaned and groaned a bit, especially when I made the critical error of coughing or twisting my body. It felt both terrifying and fascinating as my legs slowly awoke. Pain and pressure in my abdomen increased in intensity. I barely thought of my son. My disappointment was based on my obliterated expectations. My legs and brain both lay still and deadened.

Once I transitioned to our hospital room, I laid in a new, more permanent bed. A nurse adjusted my catheter and IV pole. I looked up and saw my son. Adam placed him in my arms. I didn't feel an earth-shattering shift in emotion at that moment. I just took a deep breath of my son's essence and that was good enough.

Here I was two years later in a similar situation with Skye. However, after being separated from Skye, I felt lost and confused. I tried to think reasonably and establish a plan. I would try once every hour to get up, even if I had to lie back down immediately. I took some Ibuprofen but turned down the Vicodin because I needed a clear head.

After a few futile attempts at getting up, my pain and fatigue only increased. I modified the schedule and planned an attempt for five hours hence, giving me time to sleep and eat. During this time the nurse told us that Adam could go see Skye.

He left, both of us wide-eyed at what he might see. Neither of us had much experience with hospitals, so we had no idea what the NICU entailed nor what Skye might be experiencing. I tried to sleep while he was gone. When he returned, I begged for details.

Skye had jaundice so she wore modified sunglasses over her eyes. Her head looked huge, and she wore wire leads attached to different machines. She really didn't do much when he was there. Nobody told him anything about her prognosis. He said we had to sign in to get into the NICU itself and it was on the sixth floor.

The NICU nurse told Adam that he could come back later, so he said he would return in a few hours. I told him to go up as soon as he could. If I couldn't go, at least he could see her. I forced myself to sleep so I could try to get up again and walk.

When the five-hour mark approached, Adam helped me get out of bed. Carefully placing the IV and catheter tubing out of the way, he took my hand. At a snail's pace, I inched my body to the left and attempted to bring my right shoulder up.

Fun Fact: Doing an oblique crunch with severed abdominal muscles is even harder than it sounds. Do not attempt at home, or anywhere.

After five minutes of steady progress, I forced myself to sit up the last few inches. Almost immediately, I vomited into the standard, pink plastic container the nurse gave me for this purpose. These tubs can actually be used for *any* purpose. In fact, I still have about ten of these pink tubs at my house ten years later, holding toys, cleaning supplies, and hygiene products.

Vomiting right after having abdominal surgery is an exercise in severe pain management. The vomiting reflex overtakes the body's pleas for mercy as the stomach heaves beneath freshly severed skin held together by the medical version of superglue. After hurling my guts out, I slowly laid back down. Covered in sweat, vomit, spittle, and possibly some urine, I felt like I just ran the Boston Marathon.

This time, my body left me no choice but to pass out and sleep. After waking, I made one more attempt which resulted in vomiting. But I didn't feel quite as bad, so I knew I could try again in an hour or so. I didn't vomit during the next attempt, but strong waves of nausea prevented me from taking any steps. Finally, at hour eighteen, after countless attempts, including two vomiting incidents, I stood up and took ten steps.

Adam grabbed the nurse and she assessed my vitals, watched me take steps, and called for a wheelchair. Too fatigued to make the long journey up without one, I waited impatiently for the wheelchair. When the chair arrived, I sat down in it as fast as I could. The nurse hooked the catheter tubing on the wheelchair and wrapped the IV cords around its pole so we didn't get tangled up in the process. Adam pushed my wheelchair with one hand and pulled the IV pole with his other hand, mimicking others we saw in the hospital.

We took the elevator to the sixth floor and went to the front desk. The attendant gave me a pink badge with the NICU emblem and the words "Baby Girl" printed on it. I signed the log sheet that had Adam's name scrawled on it before mine. The front desk attendant pressed a button and the NICU doors opened. Adam pushed me and the IV pole and led me to a utility sink, where we vigorously washed our hands and arms. The intense scrubbing left my arms red and sore. I would soon learn that tender arms were the least of my worries.

Chapter Seven

I smelled antiseptic cleaner and breathed sterile air. The ward had no windows so it smelled the same every single time I entered. Hospital rooms always have the same type of smell. It's a special mix of bodily fluids, IV fluids, cleaning chemicals, rubber gloves, decaying flesh, and hand sanitizer.

Every time I enter a hospital, the smell hits me immediately. Sometimes it cruelly transports me back to my time in the NICU. I am never ready for the intense, raw emotion I feel in that moment. Usually, I have to steady myself and compartmentalize. If I am alone, sometimes I cry.

On that first day in the NICU, I heard so many beeping, whirring, ringing, and humming machines that I could barely register where to look first. A long hallway branched off into a series of large rooms. I couldn't see the end rooms, but could look directly into a room simply labeled "3." Dark and quiet, it contained six incubators and rows of machines and monitors.

Adam wheeled me into a room labeled "2" and I craned my neck, looking for any sign of my baby. Adam placed my wheelchair next to an incubator and I looked inside. I saw gray jaundice glasses draped over her face, yellow skin, more leads than I could count, and a large head. My heart leapt and sank at the same time. She lived! But now she remained here in this place and I didn't know what any of it meant.

Five other incubators lined the room, each with a nametag. A nurse, changing a diaper on another baby, turned when she saw me looking at Skye.

"Hello," she said, "I assume you're mom?"

She smiled and indicated she would be with us shortly. I watched her place what looked like the world's smallest diaper on the infant. Skye looked like a toddler compared to the other baby, even though Skye was average at seven pounds, four ounces. Skye was one of the only full-term babies in the NICU. The nurses called her a giant.

The incubator had two small doors on either side, but they were closed so I wasn't sure if I could touch her. A monitor hung above her incubator, a tangled mess of wires leading from it to Skye's body. I hoped she could hear my muffled voice through the plastic box. Surely Skye felt scared and disoriented without hearing my familiar voice and heartbeat.

When the nurse finished taking care of the other infant, she came over to us. She introduced herself and said she was taking care of Skye during this shift. I asked if I could touch Skye and she said that I couldn't hold her yet, but I could gently touch her through one of the incubator doors. The nurse opened one of the doors, and I gingerly placed my hand on Skye's tiny hand and stroked it with my fingers.

"How is she?" I asked the nurse.

"Doctors have already done their rounds for the day, and I don't have a lot of information. I'm sure that one of the doctors will talk with you soon."

Skye's monitor beeped and I looked up at it anxiously. The nurse looked briefly and then silenced the alarm. "Just a blip in the lead," she said. "She's not desatting."

I learned that the pulse ox connected to Skye's foot read the oxygen saturation levels in her blood. A normal range is mid-90s to 100. When a patient's oxygen level drops lower, it warrants concern. Most of the time, it's a faulty lead or just a blip. Sometimes it leads to a "code blue," an emergency in a hospital.

Other leads measured her heart rate and respiratory rate. Each of the three rates registered as numbers with a colored waveform next to it. I watched these three waveforms and numbers as they changed every few seconds. Like the oxygen saturation levels, both heart rate and respiratory rate leads often failed or caused blips. The monitors constantly alarmed, emitting loud continuous beeps, some of which stopped on their own and some that had to be manually silenced by a nurse.

As an already anxiety-prone person, I probably aged ten years in the NICU due to my constant hypervigilance over those damn monitors. Every time an alarm sounded on Skye's monitor, I immediately glanced at it, sized up Skye, and looked around for a nurse. Sometimes a nurse came right away and sometimes I sat there for fifteen minutes with a beeping alarm inches from Skye's head, vowing to pulverize the monitor if it woke her up. Even worse, we were surrounded by other infants who all had monitors which also alarmed constantly.

Add that cacophony to the constant chatter of doctors, nurses, custodians, parents, guardians, visiting friends, specialists, and students, and it's a wonder that any baby slept for one second. Writing this almost a decade later, I can still hear the constant clanging of the monitors and see their distinctive colored waveforms.

During that first visit to the NICU, I stayed a few hours. I patted Skye's hand and watched the nurse change her diaper. I told Skye that I loved her and that I would take care of her. I honestly don't remember exactly what I felt at that moment. Everything seemed unclear and uncertain. My body and mind were still in shock and I could barely understand that the strange being in that plastic box was mine.

Chapter Eight

We rested downstairs for a few hours and then went back up to the NICU. Our assigned social worker, Alison, talked to us about living arrangements. Alison said the doctors would talk to us the next day about specifics, but we would not be leaving with Skye when I was discharged from the hospital in three days.

Our son Rowan was nearly two at the time. He had been staying with Adam's mom at her sister's L.A. house. But she had to fly back to Ohio sooner rather than later. Since we couldn't sleep in the NICU with Skye, our family would need a local place to stay while Skye remained inpatient. Alison suggested the local Ronald McDonald House.

Ronald McDonald House (RMH) is a hotel-like structure that houses families whose children are being treated at local hospitals. They are located in major cities, usually within walking distance of a children's hospital. When you see the charity box labeled Ronald McDonald House located at most McDonald's, I encourage you to throw in some change.

RMH isn't perfect, but every person who stays there has a child in their life who is sick, disabled, or dying. Sometimes people stay at RMH for months or years while their child receives cancer treatment or suffers from some sort of rare disease. People deserve to live somewhere close to the hospital during this time.

After all, who can afford a hotel room in L.A. for six months? I don't know many people who could live in L.A. and pay for the mortgage and bills back home too. If you don't think you would leave your job, your house, and your friends to go live in a strange city for months in order to get the best treatment for your kid, then you aren't human.

Big city hospitals simply have more specialists. The local hospital most likely doesn't treat babies whose intestines are born outside their bodies. It's called gastroschisis and I saw a few babies who had this birth defect. Maybe the local hospital hasn't seen a particular type of tumor. I bet the mom of the kid with the tumor does everything possible to get to the hospital that can save his life.

Adam and I agreed that Ronald McDonald House was the best fit for our family. Even though it would be a half-hour commute to the hospital, it had activities for kids, a kitchen area, and our own room with a bathroom. Alison put in the referral and told us that a room would most likely be ready when we discharged.

Luckily, we have a wonderful organization in our county called Jack's Helping Hand. It helps families like ours with medical expenses, meals, gas, and lodging. Bridget and Paul Ready selflessly started Jack's Helping Hand after their son, Jack, died of a brain tumor. They wanted families in our county to focus on their children instead of financial burdens.

Jack's Helping Hand paid for our entire Ronald McDonald House stay. They also provided various gift cards to help cover gas and groceries. I am eternally grateful to their organization and to the Ready family.

With Jack's Helping Hand providing financial assistance, Adam and I relaxed and spent more time with Skye in the NICU. We quickly learned the unwritten rules of hospital etiquette and procedure.

The next day, we went to see Skye early so we could participate in the doctor's rounds, which happen once per shift. During "rounds," the doctors, residents, charge nurse, specialists, and/or discharge nurse spend time with each patient. They view the medical chart, ask questions, give recommendations for the day, and sign orders. Orders are medical requests such as adding/editing medications, discharging patients, approving minor procedures, or modifying diet.

Nurses can't do many tasks without an order. Most nurses know exactly what needs to happen in a given situation, but their hands are tied until a doctor signs the official order. I can't tell you how many times I sat waiting on a doctor to sign an order for medication, a simple procedure, or discharge paperwork. Of course, they are busy and trying to do their best, but this paperwork process ends up causing a lot of waiting, sometimes with unpleasant results.

When the doctors came to Skye's incubator, they introduced themselves as the lead NICU physician, Dr. Danielpour, students, and fellows. The lead physician said that Skye had suffered an intraventricular hemorrhage, similar to a stroke. They spent some time trying to figure out the cause of the hemorrhage. Unfortunately, Skye developed hydrocephalus due to the hemorrhage and that then became their immediate focus.

Hydrocephalus, or water on the brain, is a buildup of too much fluid in the brain. Our brains float in our skull in a protective sac of cerebrospinal fluid (CSF). The CSF is continuously pumping and distributing itself in our spinal cord and brain. Just like a water pipe, if something blocks the pump, it can "jam" and the fluid builds up.

The fluid has nowhere to go but up and out, so a person's head enlarges. When intracranial pressure increases, it causes extreme headaches, irritability, nausea, and vomiting. A baby has a soft spot, or fontanelle, on their skull so they have more leeway for enlargement than an adult. Their heads can expand more easily. That is why Skye's head was so large when she was born. Even though her head had expanded through her fontanelle, the fluid still sat on her brain and could cause further damage.

In Skye's case, residual tissue and blood from the hemorrhage clogged up the "pipes" or ventricles. Dr. Danielpour said her brain needed to reabsorb all the blood and tissue and then we could reassess her need for any permanent procedures. But until then, he had to drain the extra fluid from her brain so it would stop causing damage and pain. He said he would place a temporary reservoir in her brain during a surgery which he had scheduled for the next day.

It was a lot of information to process and I don't remember how I integrated it into *my* brain. The biggest shock was that Skye would have surgery the next day. Dr. Danielpour asked us for consent and we signed some forms, but it didn't really feel like we had much choice. We were at Cedars-Sinai, a renowned hospital, and this is how they recommended we proceed. Adam and I aren't doctors, and I was recovering from the birth, still in my hospital gown. We signed the consent forms and looked up hydrocephalus on our phones later.

After the doctors left, I looked at Skye's small body and felt such a sense of sorrow. It was the first medical decision I made on her behalf that would cause her pain and possible side effects. I desperately wanted to switch places with her. It seemed unfathomable. She was only two days old.

Chapter Nine

The next day, I could stand and walk for longer periods of time. When they took Skye for surgery, Adam and I walked next to her gurney. She lay fairly still, ID bracelet loosely hanging on her wrist. A few nurses wheeled the gurney through a maze of elevators, heavy doors, nurse's stations, and hallways. We parted in a hallway, where I said my choked goodbye to Skye. She disappeared behind two doors and Adam and I sighed and looked at each other.

The look that passed between us at that moment has passed many times since. It's a twinkle of love, a weary shrug, a deep seed of sorrow. A mutual understanding that this moment is hard but it too shall pass.

A hospital attendant escorted us back to the elevators and told us which floor to exit and which way to turn. We made it back to the NICU and we sat in the parent room and waited. I sat on the couch next to a computer and a collection of books about parenting and birth. Adam washed his hands in a small sink and sat on a chair across from me. We sat there, playing on our phones, looking at the clock, pacing around the room. I didn't know how to feel. There wasn't a book on "How to Manage During Your Child's First Surgery" on the shelf.

It was a short procedure, so the orderlies brought Skye back up to the NICU a few hours later. She had a small bandage on the top of her head. Nothing else had obviously changed. Her color and breathing patterns had returned to baseline. She slept and I watched her chest move up and down.

Dr. Danielpour stopped by briefly and told us that everything went well. He would check in over the next few days to monitor the reservoir's progress. He explained that the reservoir didn't stop her brain from making too much fluid. It had simply been inserted in her fontanelle so the extra fluid would shoot up through it instead of sitting on her brain. Meant to be temporary, it would buy us time while the post-hemorrhagic blood and tissue reabsorbed.

"How long will the reabsorption actually take?" I asked Dr. Danielpour.

"Three to six months," he replied.

I felt like he had punched me in the throat. Six months is a long time to be sentenced to an inpatient hospital stay. I was on my third day and I already felt weary. I don't know if he felt any compassion for me, but he took a few minutes to explain the process.

Every day, a sample of her CSF would be taken through the reservoir and its protein count tested. We needed the protein level to be under 100. It had started at 530. Once the protein level decreased to under 100, we would know if she needed a permanent solution, like a shunt.

A shunt is a catheter inserted into the ventricles of the brain. A narrow tube leads down from the catheter, wraps behind the ear, and ends in the abdominal cavity. The extra CSF is deposited in the stomach and reabsorbed by the body. It's a man-made pumping system that bypasses the malfunctioning CSF system.

From that moment on, the CSF protein number became my beacon of light. I asked about the CSF number the moment I came to see Skye in the morning. That number represented when we could leave the NICU. Which also meant we could leave L.A. and the Ronald McDonald House.

During the first few days of our NICU stay, a geneticist spoke to me about her hypothesis regarding Skye's brain hemorrhage. She believed Skye had Neonatal Alloimmune Thrombocytopenia (NAIT), a disorder that affects a baby while in utero. Because of certain absent antigens in my blood, my body saw Skye as a foreign invader and attacked her platelet count.

Platelets are cells in our blood which help the clotting process. Because my body decreased Skye's platelets so low, she had uncontrolled bleeding in her brain. Her brain vessels burst and she essentially bled out. Or as my son called it, she had the "big kaboom boom."

Skye had a platelet transfusion shortly after birth, which immediately increased Skye's platelet count. To further test the NAIT hypothesis, the geneticist gave Skye an injection of IVIG, which would in theory, further increase her platelet count. Doctors took blood samples from Adam, Skye, and me and sent the samples to a lab in Wisconsin for genetic testing.

Skye's platelet count increased to normal after the blood transfusion and the IVIG infusion. It seemed likely that NAIT caused Skye's brain hemorrhage, but we had to wait for the genetic testing results to be sure.

The hospital discharged me after four inpatient days. My C-section incision looked fine and I built more endurance every day. After my discharge, Adam and I drove to Ronald McDonald House (RMH) so we could check in and get a room.

Depending on the time of day, the drive from Cedars-Sinai in Beverly Hills to RMH in East Hollywood can take twenty-five to forty minutes. Driving during the middle of the night is best for traffic, although it is much scarier to drive then.

Cedars-Sinai is in Beverly Hills, which I knew nothing about other than what Eddie Murphy taught me in *Beverly Hills Cop*. I found out that Rodeo Drive is just as fancy as it sounds, and everything is clean and crisp. Trash on the ground is nonexistent, the restaurants and stores are all expensive, and the street signs aren't askew and labeled with sarcastic and inappropriate sayings.

As I headed east out of Beverly Hills down Sunset Boulevard, I encountered narrower streets, dirtier sidewalks, and louder noises. Signs changed from Whole Foods and Pier 1 to "Hot Girls Inside" and "Vacuums fixed here. No bathroom." The makeshift homeless shelters become messier and shabbier.

This particular RMH is in a fairly seedy area of L.A. called Little Armenia. It's in East Hollywood next to Thai Town and Los Feliz. Rundown strip malls line the streets, most containing laundromats, massage parlors, smoke shops, and restaurants with sketchy names and signs. Trash lines the sidewalks and old appliances lay rotting in front yards and parking lots.

RMH Los Angeles looks exactly like a hotel, with two buildings. The front and back house are separated by a small parking area and a few houses. Since this particular RMH is in a moderately rough area, it's not a great area for leisurely walking. It has nothing to do with skin color or ethnicity. It's a bad cycle of poverty, mental illness, and unhealthy intergenerational patterns passed down. And it's L.A.

Chapter Ten

As of this writing, I have stayed at RMH Los Angeles six times for a total of seven months. I'm not saying I'm a local, but I know the area. I remain hypervigilant any time I stay there. It's similar to what I felt when I lived in Chicago in my early twenties. I imagine I'd feel the same in most big cities.

Many people living in big cities love their lives. I just don't like living that way. I prefer low-stress environments and easy navigation. I have lived in small towns for the majority of my adult life. I do miss some of the perks of big cities, like widespread public transportation and varied restaurant options.

But, in a small town, I always know how long it will take me to get to work and I always find a place to park. Drivers actually let me switch lanes in front of them and honking is rare. I know someone almost every time I go to the grocery store.

I want to be perfectly clear before I write anything else about RMH. Everyone working there wants to help others. Nonprofits don't pay well, if at all. I may complain about certain aspects of RMH, but without them, it would have been impossible for us to afford to stay by Skye. The forthcoming "complaints" of mine aren't at all the fault of the employees. They are simply results of the circumstances.

RMH holds a complicated place in my heart. It was life-saving, but also soul-sucking. It's the same way I feel about the NICU. No matter how well-intentioned the employee, those experiences traumatized me and the negative associations remain.

During that first check-in process at RMH, a staff member placed Adam and I in the back house. Our room contained two queen beds, a desk, a dresser, a chair, and a small end-table. Most importantly, each room had its own bathroom. RMH provided toilet paper, garbage bags, and laundry detergent. Rows of washers and dryers sat in the laundry room. The shared kitchen contained four ovens and four sinks with soap and drying racks. Every day, RMH provided free McDonald's coffee and cereal.

The pots, pans, measuring cups, and silverware ended up wherever the housemates decided they should go on that particular day. Most of those items had been donated so the kitchen contained a smorgasbord of dented pots, mismatched plates, and random silverware.

Different core items went missing each time I stayed there. The first time, we found only one decent pan in the cabinets. On our last stay, we found no bowls. We used the McDonald's coffee cups to eat cereal and soup. I have no idea how these items disappear. Perhaps a monster rat colony sneaks around at night and pilfers plates.

Each room received a fridge bin with a lid, a small freezer bin, and a small pantry bin. I never had anything taken during my stays. Typical for communal living, signs adorned the kitchen: "Please wash your dishes and clean up your mess." "Dirty towels don't go down the drain." "The hot water faucet is actually cold."

Meals of Love is one of the most helpful and selfless services RMH provided to its families. Local organizations or businesses in the community volunteered to come and cook a meal for the House, usually dinner. Sometimes fifteen to twenty people showed up, high energy, stoked to be helping kids and their families. Sometimes just a family of four came in and whipped up food for the masses.

Typical fare for dinners included hamburgers, spaghetti, or chicken. Huge bowls of salad, noodles, vegetables, garlic bread, cookies, cupcakes, and bottles of water lined the counter. Nothing felt more satisfying than walking in exhausted from the NICU and smelling a nice home-cooked meal. I loved grabbing those plates of food. If I lived closer, I would volunteer to do a meal there every few months. It doesn't take much to satisfy emotionally drained people.

The walls at RMH Los Angeles were thin so I could hear everything. Just like a hotel, I never knew who would stay next door to me at RMH. Wild children? Loud talkers? Insomniac tweakers? All of the above?

For the first few weeks of our stay, Adam and Rowan stayed with me. Adam and I took turns staying with Rowan, either entertaining him at RMH, or driving to various parks or malls. The other parent went to the hospital and stayed all day with Skye.

I diligently pumped breastmilk every three hours and stored the milk at the hospital. When my hospital bin filled up, I moved onto the RMH freezer. When that filled up, Jack's Helping Hand gifted us a deep freezer for home. When Adam visited on weekends, he brought a cooler which we filled to the brim with the week's breastmilk haul. With all the milk I produced, I could have fed quintuplets.

Everything felt difficult to manage, but having Adam and Rowan with me made it less so. Snuggling Rowan and processing my fears with Adam helped everything run smoother and feel easier. Later on, when they returned home, I entered a much darker emotional place.

During that first stay at RMH, a couple next door yelled and screamed, emotionally beating the crap out of each other every night. I felt especially upset because I had to wake up every three hours and pump. Already a walking zombie and completely traumatized by my days and nights in the NICU, I jolted awake when they screamed. I had such limited sleep time between pumping. I literally wanted to crash through the wall and kill them both with my bare hands, or perhaps with an RMH bath towel.

I complained to the front desk countless times, to no avail.

At that point in time, residents had to leave RMH every twenty-eight days and could return two days later. The policy existed in order to encourage a flow of people and re-establish the necessity of staying there.

We stayed with Adam's aunt for the two days, but I know other families who had to pay for a hotel on an already stretched budget. When we returned for our second cycle, RMH placed us in a different room with different neighbors. Problem solved!

This policy no longer exists and now residents can stay in the same room indefinitely. I love the change because packing up and moving out, staying somewhere random, and then moving back in two days later is emotionally draining! Especially when the stay extends to months or years. That's a lot of moving around for a stressed family.

I have never been a sound sleeper and I like things in a certain order. I hate feeling out of control. I hate when people move things around in the kitchen and I can't find them. Living in RMH felt extra difficult for me because of this control issue. I never enjoyed cooking in the kitchen because I could never find the right utensils or appliances.

Likewise, I found it difficult to survive in the NICU. I controlled nothing there. Every day, I tried not to freak out when I walked in. Doctors decided to supplement my breast milk with formula, add medications, move Skye to different rooms, and insert large needles into my daughter's brain twice a day. It all happened and I couldn't do anything about it.

A few days after Skye's reservoir surgery, I sat next to her incubator. Out of the corner of my eye, I saw her body twitch. It looked like she threw her hands up in the air as her body scrunched up into itself. I stood up and stared at her, waiting to see if it happened again. It did. I looked around nervously.

I didn't know anything about seizures at that point, but the possibility crept into my brain like a dark shadow and implanted itself. I shrugged it off and hoped it was an after-effect from her hemorrhage or the surgery itself.

After an hour, I saw it happen again, so I told the nurse. She watched and saw one herself. She made a note to tell a doctor so they could further investigate. Later that day, the head physician stopped by and told me it was very possible that Skye had a seizure. They put her on phenobarbital, an anti-seizure drug, to see if it stopped the twitching.

I thought it would be a small blip. She would be on medication for a short time and we would be done with the pesky business. I thought we had already been through so much.

Every day, a nurse pricked Skye's foot and tested her Complete Blood Count (CBC) lab levels. The CBC checked her serum sodium level, potassium level, and white and red blood cell counts, to name a few. A day after she started taking phenobarbital, Skye's serum sodium levels came back low.

I didn't understand what it meant, but the doctors considered it a serious issue. The nurses gave her a salt supplement in her bottle. The lead doctor explained to us that sodium levels can drop after surgeries. I didn't think much more about it because her serum sodium levels rose after a few days of being on the salt supplement. I had no idea what was in store.

Chapter Eleven

After a week in the NICU, a pediatric neurologist came to speak to me at Skye's bedside. She directed me to a computer work station in the back of the NICU. Bringing up images on large computer monitors, she showed me Skye's brain scans from her imaging studies.

With the MRI images, I saw Skye's brain in its entirety. With the CT scan images, I saw a dozen different slivers of Skye's brain. It looked like a finely sliced mushroom. A large, black blob covered the entire left side of Skye's brain. Her right side looked better, but it had strange white and black spots. Even my untrained eyes could see that it looked like a pretty poor excuse for a brain.

The doctor turned to me and said, "This is the worst brain hemorrhage I have ever seen." I will never forget that statement. I already knew things were bad, and I expected to see lots of issues in the brain scans. But because Skye had survived, I still felt a sense of hope.

Instead of feeling brave, I felt weak and small. Looking at that doctor, I imagined the hundreds of scans she had seen in her career. If Skye's scans were the worst she had ever seen, we were in deeper trouble than I had previously thought.

A human brain consists of two hemispheres, a left side and a right side. Each hemisphere has four symmetrical lobes, so each side is a mirror image of the other. The lobes are responsible for different jobs. For example, the occipital lobes in both hemispheres are responsible for vision. Certain jobs only exist in one hemisphere. In most people, the Broca's area, responsible for language processing, is located in the left hemisphere.

Conventional wisdom holds that logical, concrete thinkers are left-brained and that creative, artistic thinkers are right-brained. It's certainly plausible based on brain anatomy. It is, however, not a fixed science as I was soon to learn.

Skye had suffered a Grade IV hemorrhage in her left hemisphere and a Grade III hemorrhage in her right hemisphere. Grade IV is the most severe. The damage on the left side of her brain was massive, but I needed specific details to make rough predictions about future problems.

The stroke had completely destroyed the left occipital lobe. The other three left lobes looked almost entirely lost. On the "good" right side of the brain, the stroke had damaged the frontal lobe, occipital lobe, and cerebellum.

I felt my mind and body separate into two entities. My body remained seated, eyes fixated on the computer screen while my mind floated into some other space and time. I felt a hint of devastation and denial rumbling in my body, but my mind entered some sort of Lifetime movie vortex.

I wanted to believe that somebody made a mistake, that the images had been swapped with some other ones. That it had all been some sort of misunderstanding and I would be laughing with my perfect baby by the end credits.

The frontal lobe handles reasoning, impulse control, and most importantly, executive functioning. Executive functioning acts as the party planner of the brain. It oversees our higher thinking and reigns like a king over the entire critical thinking process. Without well-developed executive functioning skills, it's difficult to make sound decisions.

The occipital lobes store our visual cortex. Since both occipital lobes suffered heavy damage, I knew that Skye could be blind. For some reason, this didn't scare me as much as I thought it would. Doctors couldn't test her vision because she still wore jaundice glasses. Since we perceive most of the world visually, I felt grief for what my baby might lose. But somehow, it felt like a surmountable issue.

The majority of our brain neurons reside in the cerebellum. It controls movement, balance, and voluntary actions such as writing. An injury to the cerebellum in the first year of life is usually diagnosed as cerebral palsy. Interestingly, if the injury happens after age one, it is diagnosed as traumatic brain injury.

As we sat together at the computer screen, the pediatric neurologist diagnosed Skye with cerebral palsy due to the location of the brain damage. She remained unsure of the exact type or the degree of intensity.

I had heard of cerebral palsy, but I didn't understand exactly what it meant at the time. The pediatric neurologist said it so casually that I took it in stride and compartmentalized it for later. It wasn't as if she took my hands in hers and explained the diagnosis to me in hushed, soothing tones. I still hadn't recovered from her comments about Skye's brain and the terrible, horrible, no-good images presented to me on the computer screen.

Chapter Twelve

A day later, Adam and I attended a group meeting with Skye's hospital team. We sat around a table with physicians, specialists, surgeons, interns, and fellows. Our social worker, Alison, sat at the end of the table. Adam and I each had a pad of paper to take notes.

The lead physician spearheaded the discussion. He began by stating that no one in the room could tell us anything for sure, but they all had a general idea of Skye's future. They took turns talking about the horrible, extensive damage on both sides of her brain. No child or adult would have survived such a hemorrhage. She had miraculously survived only because she was inside me.

All the doctors agreed that she would most likely be a vegetable. They began listing off her "problems." She would never walk or talk or laugh. She would have feeding difficulties and wouldn't breastfeed. She might need a feeding tube. She would likely need anti-seizure medication for the rest of her life. She might be blind and deaf.

With each statement, I died a little more inside. I imagined Skye growing into a drooling monster with deformed limbs, a living gargoyle. Our family would never be able to leave the house. How could we take such a child with her machines and tubes and bulky wheelchair? I would be stuck at home with a vegetable forever.

Adam and I had made a list of questions before the meeting. We asked our questions, but most of them seemed pointless. We hadn't yet found out with certainty that NAIT caused her hemorrhage. The pediatric neurologist said she would take Skye off the phenobarbital in two weeks to see if the twitching subsided.

The general plan was to keep her inpatient in the NICU until her CSF proteins dropped below 100. If Dr. Danielpour determined she needed a shunt, he would surgically implant it into Skye's brain and discharge her a few days post-surgery. The doctors all reiterated that Skye would be inpatient for another three to six months.

After the meeting, our social worker, Alison, took us to a private room where the three of us cried together. I don't remember much of what anyone said, because what is there to say? I felt hopeless and helpless.

I kept thinking about a day right before my midwife called me about the mass on Skye's brain. Adam and I played Wii bowling in our living room. We stood next to each other, furiously moving our controllers, bumping into each other, and laughing hysterically. Rowan sat on the couch behind us, squealing with delight every time one of us knocked down the pins. I touched my belly constantly. I knew our daughter would be joining us shortly and I smiled with pure joy.

It is the last memory I have of my old life.

I'm not the most optimistic person. But I had no choice other than to keep moving. After the horrific team meeting, I clung to any shard of hope available. My daughter had suffered a massive brain hemorrhage that permanently damaged her brain. However, due to the concept of neuroplasticity, the healthy parts of Skye's brain could pick up some of the slack.

Neuroplasticity is a fancy term for the brain's ability to form new neural connections and take over functions of damaged parts.

Scientists used to think that each part of the brain had one function, so brain damage destroyed skills or abilities forever. Now, scientists know that if one part of the brain is damaged, healthy neurons can rewire to compensate for lost skills or abilities.

The brain's motto is, "Use it or lose it." This concept applies to anyone's brain, healthy or not. The brain is constantly pruning old neurons and forming new ones. Most of the rapid growth and change occurs when people are young. However, a person of any age remains capable of some neuroplastic change.

As cliché as it sounds, it really is never too late to teach an old dog new tricks. In fact, stimulating the brain while aging is the best way to keep it healthy. Doing crossword puzzles, learning a new language, playing trivia games, or taking a college class are all ways to keep an older brain vibrant. Learning something new forces the brain to expand and work. Old information gets thrown out.

Gardeners prune small or dead branches on plants in order for the plants to experience new, healthy growth. Likewise, the brain prunes old, dead neurons and focuses on core functions.

If I take guitar lessons, parts of my brain rewire and grow in size. That helps my brain hold onto that new skill. Every time I practice, those neurons grow bigger and stronger. Weirdly, even visualizing myself playing a guitar chord increases the size of that area in the brain.

However, other skills I don't practice start fading away and lose space in my brain. These skills aren't necessarily lost, but the brain deems them less important. Even though I took years of Spanish classes, I have lost much of my skill because I don't speak the language regularly.

The system isn't perfect. Sometimes functions become permanently lost. Sometimes functions reappear at random times. Sometimes functions come back, aren't used often enough, and then disappear again. Some functions have a harder time than others with the compensation process, such as motor function, visual function, and language function.

For a more scientific and better explanation of neuroplasticity, I suggest Norman Doidge's *The Brain That Changes Itself*. It is a fabulous read for anyone who has a brain or knows someone who does.

Chapter Thirteen

Most of the women in the NICU had C-sections. Some happened by choice, but most happened suddenly. I knew two moms in the NICU who gave birth when they were twenty-four weeks pregnant. A first-time mom barely looks pregnant at that stage.

One baby only weighed fifteen ounces at birth, less than a pound. The baby looked like a shriveled prune.

These small babies are so fragile that even their mothers can't hold them or take them out of the incubator for weeks. I felt heartbroken watching baby Hudson's mom sit in her rocking chair next to his incubator and wait. I believe she waited a month before she held him.

The five rooms in the Cedars-Sinai NICU progressed from level one to level five. The rooms didn't always equate to a baby's level of imminent danger because a NICU, like any other hospital ward, plays a daily game of Tetris with beds, patients, ventilators, monitors, fluid poles, and chairs. It never ends.

However, a general system dictated the ward. Level one usually meant the baby had serious issues and level five held stable babies close to discharge. In those upper level rooms, nurses could take care of three babies at a time versus the lower levels where a nurse cared for only two babies at a time.

When a baby moved to an upper level and showed signs of

stability (no baby is ever truly stable in the NICU by definition), the family could breathe a little lighter. After all, they might just actually make it out of there with a live baby. The mom might dare a smile while scrubbing her arms and hands in the industrial sink, humming a tune beneath her breath, absentmindedly touching her hospital bracelet that had become permanent jewelry.

The nurses moved Skye five times when she stayed there, which is a pain – unless Skye moved to a more stable room or closer to one of my friends. It was always wonderful to see a familiar face in that chaotic world, especially with all the transient traffic. I greeted the nurses and other moms like they were my family, because in that situation, they were the only people who mattered.

> **Fun Fact:** Stevie Wonder was born with normal eyes and
> brain structures, but the doctors placed him in an
> incubator with too much oxygen and he lost his vision.

I could tell the new parents immediately. The scenario was always the same: a woman riding up in a wheelchair, shuffling along like a ninety-year-old. She'd wear a hospital gown loosely tied over sweatpants, and had eyes wide as saucers. She had just learned that her baby had a problem and she now resided in the world of the NICU. Would this new mother be lucky and get out in three days? Or would she become a lifer, like me?

One mom had a baby boy who had swallowed some meconium (baby poop), so the doctors placed him in the NICU to be monitored until he regained stability. She told the nurses not to feed her baby because she wanted to exclusively breastfeed. She told them she would arrive every three hours until the hospital discharged her son.

I both admired the mom and hated her. She had every right to breastfeed exclusively and, in theory, it should have been possible. If the baby only stayed for a few days, the mother would still be inpatient in the hospital. Since she had a vaginal birth, she would regain her mobility almost immediately. Every three hours, she could meander upstairs, check in at the front desk, scrub up, feed her baby, then meander down to her room again to sleep. Her baby might cry sometimes, but he would survive.

I hated the mom's guts because her baby had such a minor, routine issue and she could be so steadfast in her convictions. Our babies lived on different planes of existence. I had no choice but to relinquish control over bottles, formula, feeding times, and expectations of my mammary glands and my child's whims. That mom and her baby left after a few days and she did manage to breastfeed her son exclusively. I still detest her.

I played the role of "scary mom," although I also gave many people hope. One of the first questions I got from a new mom was always, "How long have you been here?" I would take a deep breath, stand up a little taller, and say "two weeks," or, "six weeks," or at the end, "ninety-six days."

I observed the look of horror that I saw on many parents' faces after I told them, especially toward the end of our stay. Obviously, it lends itself to thinking - my God, could that happen to me? Will my baby be that sick? And often, what in the hell is wrong with your kid?

When the hospital discharged babies from the NICU, nurses placed the baby in a blue buggy. Caretakers pushed the buggy while a nurse escorted them to their car. Whenever a blue buggy swooped by, I felt happy for the baby and their caregivers. But it always made me sadder, especially at first, when I knew we wouldn't be out for three to six months.

Many days I felt tempted to rip off Skye's leads, pick her up and run and run until I made it all the way home. But it's actually a crime to do so. Because Skye had never come home, the hospital had legal sway over her care. So even though it was my baby, it wasn't my final decision about what happened to her. That's why I had to let some of their decisions go. I couldn't fight every battle or I wouldn't win the war.

It proved difficult to hold Skye with so many leads attached to her body. I couldn't snatch her up when she cried and throw her on the breast. I had to complete an intricate dance of untangling wires and maneuvering my arms and torso around like a drunk contortionist. Sometimes I needed a nurse's assistance, especially early in our NICU experience.

At first, I had the terrible idea that if I unplugged one of the leads, the whole system would collapse. After a few weeks, and even now when I go to hospitals, I readjust the oxygen desat lead if it's not reading, silence alarms on monitors, or find a nurse if necessary. Nurses spend their busy days helping other patients or taking breaks. If the beep doesn't constitute an emergency, no one is running to turn them off. Nothing pisses me off more than a nonstop beeping alarm sitting two feet away from my mercifully sleeping baby.

Since I know every person reading this who works in a hospital is about to wring my neck, let me say that patients should not do this. Proper behavior demands that a patient or family member should just sit and wait for help. It is not a good idea to mess around with monitors.

When I had Rowan, I placed him in a baby carrier on my chest. He snuggled next to me for his entire first year of life. He cried when we put him in the crib, and would only take naps lying on or next to an adult. When I look back at that first year of his life, I cherish the ease of those moments. Although it seemed difficult, it was such a sweet and innocent time.

In Skye's case, I had to come to terms with the fact that I wouldn't be walking around with my daughter snuggled next to me in a baby carrier. I also wouldn't be lying next to her, breastfeeding her to sleep.

When I brought a moby wrap in (a baby carrier made out of fabric), I had to get permission from three different people in order to even attempt to use it in the NICU. I tried on multiple occasions, but the leads kept getting snagged and I had to redo the whole contraption over and over. Skye has never exhibited much patience, so I became flustered when she screamed and fussed while I got us settled. I gave up after a few tries.

When the doctor finally removed Skye's jaundice glasses, I stared deep into her eyes looking for abnormalities. She didn't look at anything in particular. Weirdly, her eyes darted back and forth, like a pendulum on speed. I asked when her vision could be checked and the nurse made a note for the doctors.

Within a few days, a pediatric ophthalmologist came and examined her eyes. He used various implements to test her eyesight.

"Your daughter has nystagmus but she has no ocular issues."

"What's nystagmus?"

"Nystagmus is a visual impairment that causes the eyes to move irregularly. Sometimes it causes acuity issues or problems with coordination. She isn't blind. I'm writing that she's 20/20 on her chart."

Even though the doctor wrote 20/20 on her chart, he didn't convince me. Even though an infant's eyes lack focus, they will track objects and look into their caregiver's eyes. I bored a hole into Skye's soul with how intensely I stared into her eyes. She didn't react. I moved shiny, bright objects around her head and she didn't react. I knew her eyes weren't working well, but I didn't understand the exact problem.

When I told the doctors my lingering concerns, they looked at the chart and showed me the ophthalmologist's note.

"It shows that Skye's eyesight is 20/20," the doctors said.

"I know what it says," I replied, "but he has to be wrong."

The doctors shrugged their shoulders. "This ophthalmologist works at Cedars-Sinai Medical Center," their shrugs said. "Who are you to disagree?"

Chapter Fourteen

Throughout the next few weeks, Skye didn't look at anything. I considered her blind. I felt upset that no one else believed me. None of the doctors or nurses could get past the ophthalmologist's note.

Everyone agreed that she wasn't looking at anything. However, at that point, Skye was fairly unresponsive in general. I think everyone assumed any issues were because of her "vegetative" state.

I never let it go. I bugged the doctors and nurses about it so much that the ophthalmologist came back twice more to examine her. Both times he reported the same findings: Skye's ocular structures tested as normal and the nystagmus wouldn't cause complete blindness.

I felt like a hysterical patient, locked in a straitjacket and dragged away to a padded room while screaming, "I'm not crazy! I'm not crazy!" I'm sure I annoyed both the staff and doctors. I wasn't trying to provoke hysteria. I knew something was very wrong with Skye's vision.

Skye writhed around, never seemed settled, and whined instead of cooing. The doctors told Adam and me that Skye might exhibit a neurological irritability forever. They described the irritability as high-pitched screaming and whining with a general presentation of discomfort and unhappiness. We anticipated a screaming, raging vegetable.

I struggled with such a disheartening reality. Adam and I didn't talk about it at that point. Adam rarely engages in hypothetical assumptions. He waits for reality to present itself first. I find it annoying.

I desperately wanted to talk about my fears and feelings. I didn't have many people to choose from. I excluded anyone who hadn't raised kids, my friends raising typical kids, and Adam's mom, because she struggled with her own grief. That didn't leave many options.

I spent more time with Skye than anyone else and I saw brief moments of lucidity. When I mentioned Skye's moments of calmness and cooing, doctors reminded me of the initial prognosis of doom. The doctors couldn't provide me false hope, but I felt like a little girl patted on the head by the "adults" in the room. Skye's lucid behaviors only lasted for a few moments at a time. I fell into despair when she returned to being unresponsive.

In terms of her irritability, I reminded everyone that she probably suffered great pain and discomfort. The temporary reservoir in her brain collected extra cerebralspinal fluid and shot it up between her fontanelles. When the fluid collected there, her scalp stretched and expanded. It literally looked like she had a softball sticking up from the top of her head.

The intense pressure of the extra fluid sat on top of her head all the time. In addition, she had recently suffered a massive brain hemorrhage. No wonder she exhibited irritability!

After a month in the NICU, Dr. Danielpour told me that Skye needed a reservoir revision surgery. Scar tissue blocked the reservoir and it would cause problems if he didn't go in and clean it up. He described the surgery as quick and easy with low risks.

I consented to the surgery and Dr. Daniepour operated within a few days. Everything went well during surgery and the size of the fluid atop her head decreased in size. After two brain surgeries, I started to feel like a pro!

However, within a week of the surgery, Skye's blood serum sodium levels came back as low again. This time, they dropped quickly so the doctors expressed more concern. They called in a urologist and he talked to me about Skye possibly having (get ready!) "Syndrome of Inappropriate Antidiuretic Hormone Secretion (SIADH)." This syndrome has various causes, but it essentially means that the body secretes too much of an antidiuretic hormone called AVP.

The doctor wasn't sure if Skye had the syndrome, but he gave me an article he wrote about SIADH. He planned to follow her case for a few weeks to see how she reacted to the salt supplement given in her breast milk. If that didn't increase the sodium levels, he would suggest some alternative treatments outlined in the article. I scanned the article and looked up some additional information online. The information scared and confused me because of all the potential long-term problems and issues.

At that same time, I received more devastating news. Rowan and Adam had to leave L.A. and return home, four hours away. Adam had to return to work. Someone had to pay the mortgage and the bills. Life didn't stop because we had a sick kid. Since no one under the age of twelve is allowed to enter the NICU, I couldn't keep Rowan with me and visit Skye simultaneously.

We made the difficult decision for Adam to take Rowan home and put him in full-time daycare. I would stay behind at RMH and the two of them would drive down every weekend possible. I hated the thought of Rowan attending full-time daycare.

I knew that plenty of kids attended full-time daycare, but we had worked hard to keep him home part-time. I hated that he would be raised by strangers while his mother and baby sister remained in a different part of the state. We couldn't think of any other scenario, so I had to let it happen and deal.

Rowan was almost two at the time. I looked at his sweet smile and felt the world crumble beneath me. Having him around acted as a buffer from the horror and fear all around me. Unsure of Skye's survival or eventual future, I craved the certainty of my typical child and his capable mind and body. Watching him run around and hearing his voice and the pitter-patter of his tiny feet gave me some of my only sources of solace. To be separated from him seemed unfathomable.

Adam is a fabulous father, so it helped alleviate some fears. Even without me, Rowan would be safe and loved. But I worried about Rowan's attachment to me and our mother-son relationship. Every day he seemed to change. Would he forget about me during the time we were separated? Would we grow apart? Would he feel sad? I almost couldn't breathe thinking about how I would manage.

I had no choice. I still feel guilty about that time of separation, and I always wonder if it negatively affected him. Now at age eleven, Rowan is the most independent kid I know. Much of this independence is probably natural, but years of getting dragged around to various hospitals and months of separation from me certainly helped forge his path.

He has spent long days entertaining himself, watching his parents freak out, and listening to his sister scream in pain. He knows more about hospitals and serious medical issues than most adults. He has stayed in countless hotels and unfamiliar homes with random friends and relatives. The NICU stint was our first separation. Unfortunately, it wouldn't be our last.

Chapter Fifteen

When Rowan and Adam left, I entered a dark place. Depression had been an acquaintance of mine, but we became close friends for the rest of my NICU stay. I have plenty of energy and drive so I managed to fake it while interacting with the world. As much as I wanted to avoid the NICU and the reality of Skye's severe issues, I couldn't wallow in my bed, crying about the unfairness of life.

So, I pushed my horrible, awful, scary thoughts to some secret drawer deep in my subconscious. I knew that I would have to open the drawer and deal with its contents at some point, but I had more important things to focus on. Each morning I forced myself to shower, eat, and put on deodorant. I continued the daily commute between Ronald McDonald House and Cedars-Sinai.

On a typical day I'd wake up at RMH and pump with a borrowed hospital-grade breast pump. The suction squeezed both breasts so that I could express milk into bottles attached to my nursing bra (yes, it's like milking a cow). I poured the expressed milk into special ziplock bags and labeled them with the date and amount. The bags went into the freezer for later use. I washed the bottles and breast shields in my bathroom sink and left them to dry.

I usually ate a quick breakfast of cereal and coffee at RMH. I drove down Beverly Blvd. and turned left onto La Cienega Blvd. toward hospital parking. I had all the right badges and bracelets, so I could enter the hospital and go right up to the sixth floor. I checked in at the NICU front desk, signed my name on the logbook, and waited to be buzzed in.

After scrubbing my arms and hands, I entered Skye's room and greeted the nurse. I grabbed a chair and breastfeeding stool, which were few and far between for some reason. Since there were rarely more than one or two other parents visiting their infants in each individual ward, I could usually snag one.

I said hello to Skye and looked at her monitor to make sure there weren't any irregularities. If she was asleep, I'd sit quietly until the nurse came over to give me an update. If she was awake, I stroked her hands and legs and talked to her. At first, she didn't sit up or move much so she lay on her back, staring up at seemingly nothing. She still wasn't turning her head or responding to noises.

The nurse came over and let me know any pertinent information about Skye's night. Since Skye was a "lifer," the hospital assigned her a primary day nurse and a primary night nurse. These nurses worked directly with Skye. The continuity of care could really improve the outcome for such complex infants.

Two shifts exist in a hospital: day shift and night shift. During the switch, the outgoing nurse gives the incoming nurse updates and information on each patient. I recommend not needing anything during the switch if you want to keep the nurses on your good side.

Helpful Hint: You definitely *do* want nurses on your good side. And all other hospital personnel.

Skye's day nurse, Nancy, was nice but no-nonsense. She had decades of experience and she treated Skye well. Tall with blond hair and long arms and legs, Nancy towered over the other nurses. She never hesitated to tell doctors or other nurses that they needed to do something immediately.

Skye's night nurse, Heather, was warm and giving, and also had decades of nursing experience. Her beautiful brown skin reminded me of smooth chocolate, and she had long black hair and high cheekbones. Her smile seemed genuine, and I felt at ease around her.

I either pumped or breastfed every three hours, depending on the day. At first, the nurses bottle-fed Skye with a combination of my pumped breastmilk and some supplemental formula. As she grew and became more responsive, Skye breastfed at times. If she acted too lethargic or wasn't latching on the breast, the nurse bottle-fed my breastmilk.

Over time, Skye gained strength and I gained experience. I started changing her diapers and giving her bottles. This allowed the nurses to focus on the more complicated tasks of administering medications, adjusting leads, and completing their never-ending pile of charting.

Nurses (and most other hospital personnel) complete an inordinate amount of paperwork during each shift. Every action must be written or typed in the patient's chart. Keeping track of patient treatments and meds obviously needs to be done, but endless, menial paperwork seems to take away from direct patient care.

Obviously the hospital needs accountability and effective practices. Liability remains a huge issue. Patients and families sue doctors and hospitals. Nurses should track medication, general observations, doctor's orders, and specialist recommendations. However, many of the redundancies could be eliminated. Nurses type the same information about the same patient daily, or sometimes even hourly.

The problem is complex, and I am obviously not privy to administrative decisions. However, I wish nurses could spend less time charting and more time with patients and families.

Even with systemic problems and charting burnout, nurses and doctors meticulously cared for Skye and kept her alive. I continued my daily grind and spent as much time as I could with Skye and the friends I made among other "lifer" moms.

After six weeks, the genetic testing came back positive for NAIT. We now knew the official cause of her brain hemorrhage. Even though I felt needlessly guilty for being the parent with screwed-up antigens, I felt a huge sense of relief. I didn't eat the wrong food or exercise too aggressively. The doctors didn't act in a negligent manner.

The geneticist explained that if we became pregnant again, the same problem would develop with the incompatible antigens. The doctors could try to prevent the problem. I could take Prednisone, IVIG shots, and have the baby taken prematurely at about thirty-two weeks. The protocol sounded tough, but doable. However, the odds that this could happen again were too high. Adam and I talked and decided that we were done having babies.

We had two children already and I was thirty-four. One of the children was a very ill infant who wasn't looking great at the moment. We cut our proverbial losses and Adam literally "cut" something as well.

Knowing what caused Skye's hemorrhage is a luxury. Many parents never know. A good friend of mine traveled to Stanford doing test after test in order to learn why her child had neurological issues. She only recently found an answer, fifteen years later. Having additional children becomes an anxiety-fueled nightmare. The lifelong what-ifs circle the brain like vultures.

Chapter Sixteen

Many parents visited the NICU regularly. But some babies had parents who didn't visit much and a few babies never had visitors. Many local parents worked and took care of their other children, so I understood why they only came for a few hours after dinner or maybe every other day.

I went to the NICU every single day. Sometimes I stayed until midnight. I saw everything. I spent hours sitting idly in a chair, trying to be relatively quiet. Cell phones were discouraged, and cell phone conversations were prohibited. Wi-Fi service worked intermittently and glitched out, so I spent most of my time people-watching.

I sat across from one baby's incubator for weeks. The baby had been born prematurely and seemed like he had breathing issues. I looked over at him quite often. I watched this baby lie on his back in his incubator while his breathing apparatus helped him stay alive. The nurses checked on him. They changed his diapers and fed him. Doctors completed rounds each morning and spoke of his progress or lack thereof. Nurses updated his charts.

But for the longest time, he had not one visitor. It saddened me every day when no one came in to see him. I heard the nurses gossip about the parents. I fantasized about who they might be. Teenage parents who couldn't handle it? A shamed family who couldn't culturally accept a son with medical issues? Addicts? Abject poverty? Field workers who simply couldn't take the time off?

One day when I entered the NICU, the baby's parents stood next to his incubator talking with the lead physician. I felt incredulous. They were a well-dressed couple in their thirties. They looked like ordinary folks I wouldn't notice in a crowd. I couldn't hear most of their conversation, but the end result was that their son would be in the NICU for some time. The nurses moved Skye to a different room one week later. I never saw the parents again.

Different contextual circumstances might explain why parents would essentially abandon their child in a hospital. Plenty of cultural, medical, emotional, and psychological reasons exist for parents not spending time with their sick infant. I had the privilege of being emotionally and financially stable. Even though it almost broke me, I could spend time with Skye every day. However, I still can't understand this one family's absence.

During my stay in the NICU, the parents I met all lived locally. Every mother and father went home each night and maintained a semi-normal life. They spent time with their friends, worked, ate at their own dining room table, and slept in their own beds. Many parents had daily visits from friends, co-workers, and family. I wouldn't say they lived a "normal" life *per se*, but they lived with buffers and supports.

My friend Anika's mother sat by her side nearly every day. They spoke fervent Spanish to each other, and laughed and hugged each other. Her mother assisted Anika during pumping by bagging up her breastmilk and washing the pumping equipment. Having a wing-woman throughout the process must have been fabulous for Anika. Each night she and her mother returned to their home, a short drive away. Even though Anika became my closest friend in the NICU, I felt insanely jealous.

Watching Anika and her mother interact became excruciating for me. Even if my mother were alive, I doubt she would have moved to California for months to be with me. But even from afar, her strength and intelligence would have benefited both Skye and me. I desperately wanted my mother's reassurance that everything would be okay.

I already missed my mother, but the NICU experience intensified my longing for her. Even when I feel sick as an adult, I crave nothing more than my mom tucking me into bed and feeding me chicken noodle soup. Everyone regresses when they feel scared and sick, and it's no different during emotional crises.

After Rowan and Adam left, I had good days and bad days. It was pretty simple. If Skye had a good day, I had a good day. If she had a bad day, I had a bad day. I kept to my routine as much as possible. I ate lunch at the same restaurants in Beverly Hills and took the same elevators in the hospital. I drove the same way to and from the hospital and RMH.

I never did anything else even though I lived in L.A. Adam's family stayed busy with their own lives. I didn't know anyone else and I felt too tired and sad to care. My skin looked pale from spending all day inside and I hadn't lost a single pound since the day I gave birth. My stomach jiggled and hung over my pants and I felt like crap about it. I wore loose, baggy clothing and large nursing bras. I struggled to apply moisturizer and put my hair into a loose ponytail. In addition, I had to pump every three hours. This schedule didn't leave much time for cocktail hour.

Meanwhile, on the medical front, the doctors removed the phenobarbital from Skye's daily regimen after a few weeks. The neurologist didn't talk to me about long-term medication so I assumed Skye's twitching activity had been an anomaly. She didn't share with me that doctors had performed an electroencephalogram

(EEG), a test that looks at the electrical activity in the brain.

I only saw years later when I looked through Skye's medical records that the NICU doctors conducted an EEG and found abnormal brain wave activity. Since I wasn't informed of this at the time, I didn't give it another thought during our stay.

Over time, the bubble of fluid on Skye's head grew bigger and bigger. When the fluid expanded, the situation became dangerous. If too much pooled up, it could cause further brain damage. Also, as the bubble of fluid grew larger, Skye became more irritable. She would fuss and scream and moan and groan while I tried desperately to calm her by singing and stroking her legs and arms.

Dr. Danielpour talked to me about the need to "tap" the fluid daily. A doctor would insert a large needle into the reservoir in her brain and withdraw the fluid. After the tap, the bubble of fluid would deflate, much like an old balloon. Only a neurosurgeon or the neurosurgical fellows could perform the tapping.

Every time the bubble grew abnormally large, the nurses had to page neurosurgery. The fluid could expand quickly and sometimes the pages would go unanswered. The nurses would wait an hour and page again. If the fluid increased rapidly, the nurses would page every twenty minutes. I had no choice but to sit and wait, soothing an extremely irritable baby, and dreaming of the myriad ways I would kill the neurosurgeons (after they tapped her, of course).

I hate even thinking about the tapping process. It isn't natural to watch a large needle enter anyone's head. When the neurosurgeons entered Skye's head with the needle, they created risk. I watched most of those daily taps with trembling hands and sweat dripping down my back and face.

A nurse held Skye down and the neurosurgical fellow painstakingly marked a spot on her head and inserted the needle. The fellow slowly drew the needle up and away and deposited the fluid in a jar. Skye became dysregulated and upset during the process and I had to watch from afar.

After a few weeks of daily taps, Dr. Danielpour told me that Skye would need to be tapped twice a day. I probably grabbed onto the nearest chair so I didn't faint. The reservoir was barely doing its job and was maxing out. Her protein counts still weren't low enough for shunt placement. More tapping meant more pain, more frustration, and more irritability. It also meant more waiting for someone to show up and tap her.

One night Skye's fluid pooled rapidly. In a matter of fifteen minutes, the bubble on top of her head became absurdly large. Skye fussed and cried nonstop. The nurse and I looked at each other and she immediately paged neurosurgery. Minutes passed and Skye cried louder. The nurse paged every five minutes, both of us desperately trying to soothe Skye. I tried not to panic. I felt terrified at how quickly the bubble grew. I remembered Dr. Danielpour's ominous warnings about further brain damage.

We grabbed the charge nurse and told her about the situation. She paged the neurosurgeons too. After an eternity, a group of doctors entered the room. I had never seen any of these doctors before, which struck me as strange.

One doctor looked at Skye and asked the nurse to assist. Skye writhed in pain. The doctor fumbled with the needle and the tubing. His hands shook. I looked at the nurse but she held Skye in position. He made a mark on her head. He inserted the needle and he missed the mark. Skye screamed and he cursed, taking the needle out. Blood covered the needle.

"Hold her steady," he barked.

He inserted the needle for the second time and he missed the mark. The needle looked even bloodier. The needle had never been bloody before when anyone else tapped the reservoir. Was he poking her brain? The nurse demanded someone else tap her.

"There is no one else," he said.

I stood frozen in place, trapped in my own body. I should have stepped in and told him to stop and demanded he find someone else anyway. However, if no one else could come (absolutely possible since it took so long for them to arrive), it was probably better that the hack doctor try one more time. I watched the incompetence in a dissociative state, as if it were happening to someone else. I couldn't move. I couldn't speak. I couldn't form a complete thought.

Mercifully, he hit the mark on his third try. Everyone sighed in relief. Still in shock, I watched him take off his gloves and carry the jar of Skye's brain fluid out of the room. I somehow managed to move my legs and ran to Skye's bedside. I tried to comfort her but I could barely function. I don't know to this day if he caused more brain damage. I still feel like a bad mother because I shut down when it mattered most.

Chapter Seventeen

I spoke to Dr. Danielpour about the incident the next day so he knew that he had an incompetent doctor on his team who obviously needed more training. I asked that the fellow never come again. Dr. Danielpour said he had no idea who the doctor was and that he wasn't one of his fellows.

"Then who was he?" I asked.

"Probably a doctor on call," he said.

He didn't seem too concerned about the bloody needle. In the grand scheme of his cases, it probably didn't seem like a big deal to him.

Every once in a while, when Skye experiences a medical crisis, I wonder if the hack doctor caused that particular problem. Did his fishing around exacerbate an already horrific situation? I don't know for sure and there certainly isn't anything I can do about it now.

After two and a half months, Skye's CSF protein count finally decreased to 100. Dr. Danielpour told me that if the count continued to decrease for a few more days, he would schedule the surgery to insert a VP shunt (ventriculoperitoneal shunt).

After Skye's birth, Dr. Danielpour told Adam and me that her hydrocephalus could clear up and her brain would reset. Once I saw the massive amounts of CSF pooling up in her head each day, I knew the hydrocephalus wasn't clearing up on its own. I accepted the fact that she needed a permanent solution.

Shunt technology hasn't changed much in sixty years. It's not a great system. The shunt can malfunction at any second. It can be a life or death emergency. If Skye's shunt fails and we don't get her to a pediatric neurosurgeon quickly enough, she can suffer more brain damage or death. The signs of a shunt malfunction include lethargy, excessive vomiting, and irritability.

Sometimes a person's shunt suffers continual malfunctions and infections. Some people have had forty shunt surgeries. Sometimes a person has only one shunt for decades with no problems. As of this writing, Skye still has the same shunt that Dr. Danielpour inserted in the NICU.

Unfortunately, Skye is a puker. She takes after Adam, who vomits on boats, in cars, on spinning rides, and sometimes for seemingly no reason at all. Her damaged brain, bad genetics, probable migraine-like headaches, and visual impairments lead to lots of random vomiting. And not unexpectedly, when she vomits, she tends to be irritable and tired.

If I even suspect Skye's shunt might be malfunctioning, I have to take her immediately to the nearest ER. The doctors perform a shunt series, which consists of X-rays of her brain and the entire tubing system. Sometimes the tubing can tangle or become clogged up. Sometimes the catheter moves out of place. Sometimes the setting changes unexpectedly.

A VP shunt has a programmable setting that can change if the person comes into contact with a magnet. Examples of problematic magnets include airport security booths, iPads, Thomas the Train engines, and MRIs. I don't know that a regular fridge magnet is strong enough to cause a problem, but we are careful nevertheless. The magnet isn't a problem if it stays at least two inches away from the catheter in her brain.

We have chosen to avoid the airport security booth and request a pat-down check for Skye instead. TSA workers usually don't know what we mean when we say she has a shunt, but anyone by law can request a pat-down so they comply. When she has an MRI, we request an X-ray series both before and after to make sure the setting is correct and her tubing remains in place.

I hate the fact that she will need a piece of equipment in her brain forever. As of today, nothing better exists for the treatment of hydrocephalus, and shunts can't be removed without risk of death. However, if the hydrocephalus remains untreated, the patient's head continues to grow.

Without a shunt placement, a hydrocephalic patient's head can grow to the size of a watermelon. They have to lie down at all times and most likely have the world's worst headache. In many countries, shunt surgeries are commonplace. In some countries, pediatric neurosurgeons aren't readily available and surgery is exorbitantly expensive.

Mercifully, Dr. Danielpour came to rounds a few days later and said that Skye's protein count had dipped below 100. He scheduled her shunt surgery for the following Monday. I ran out of the NICU and called Adam. Adrenaline and elation coursed through me. I tried hard to regain my composure. The nurses and other moms expressed their joy for Skye and me. I would finally get to sleep in my own bed and see my friends! It had seemed elusive for so long.

Adam and Rowan drove down to the hospital so we could spend a few days together before the surgery. I felt nervous, but I felt more excited about going home. We spent our time playing at Ronald McDonald House and packing up some of our belongings. I texted all our family and friends and sent them a picture of Skye. I captioned the picture, "If all goes well, we should be home in a few days."

Everyone responded with warm, encouraging words and emojis.

My grandmother started a prayer chain at her church so a few hundred strangers in Pennsylvania prayed for us.

The night before the surgery, Adam and Rowan fell asleep easily. It annoyed me that Adam could close his eyes so quickly. In true form, I tossed and turned and ruminated. I thought about death and life and what-ifs and more what-ifs. At some point, my body shut down and I slept.

I woke to a strange buzzing sound, something so subtle that I couldn't discern its origin. I looked around the room, darkness shrouding my vision. Even after months in the RMH rooms, everything remained unfamiliar, with jutting corners and ominous shadows. Obviously in the middle of the night, somewhere vaguely strange, something was bothering me awake.

It hit me and I jumped up. My cell phone was ringing! I ran to it but I didn't make it in time. The NICU phone number showed up as a missed call. I dialed it and waited on hold while Adam groggily woke up. Rowan lay still in his bed, oblivious. The front desk put me through to a nurse practitioner in the NICU. She had spent a lot of time with Skye and myself over the last few weeks.

Our conversation went something like this:

"Uh, we have a situation here with Skye. It's her sodium levels again." She sounded somber. "We are figuring it out, but I don't know what will happen." She spoke slowly and deliberately. She didn't want me to panic and she probably felt terrified.

"Do I need to come in now or should I wait until the morning when we come in for surgery?" I asked.

"Skye won't be having surgery tomorrow," she said.

It was something like two in the morning. I felt confused. My brain wasn't handling reality.

"You might want to get some more sleep and come in a few hours. Surgery isn't possible when sodium is low. Skye needs to stabilize first."

"Okay," I mumbled, knots forming in my stomach.

"Come soon, though," she said.

We said our goodbyes and I hung up. I conveyed the message to Adam.

I felt disappointed and helpless. All my excitement and elation floated away. Exhausted and weary, Adam and I decided we should try to sleep. We had dealt with low sodium before and we would deal again. Her surgery would be rescheduled soon, maybe in a few days. I didn't understand the gravity of the situation.

Chapter Eighteen

When I entered the NICU the next morning, I saw a cluster of doctors gathered around Skye. I had never seen more than two doctors by her bedside before. A fiery ball of terror arose in my stomach and I ran to her incubator. She had an IV inserted in her hand, but that was standard practice for Skye. I didn't see anything else concerning. The doctors all turned to me with morose expressions, and one of them began talking in a hushed tone.

"Skye's sodium is very low. It's a remarkably low number actually. It's 99, which I've never seen in my career." The doctor looked incredulous as he spoke. Everyone did. Once again, my child existed as a medical marvel. She became the freak show for everyone to study.

"What does that mean? What's happening to her?"

I knew that normal sodium levels ranged from 135-145 so 99 sounded really bad.

"The protocol for raising her sodium levels is to give her an intravenous sodium solution. We'll increase the dosage at a slow, precise rate over two weeks." He breathed unevenly. "Even so, she could experience hyponatremic encephalopathy."

Fun Fact: Hyponatremic encephalopathy can result in catastrophic brain damage, seizures, or permanent breathing issues.

"Will she die?" I asked.

The doctor looked at his colleagues. They shifted and averted their eyes.

"I don't know. Most people don't make it to 99 before lapsing into a coma. This is uncharted territory here." He shrugged and I clenched my hands into fists.

I couldn't fathom why I didn't drive to the NICU when the nurse practitioner called. I should have listened to the fear in her voice instead of getting three more hours of sleep. I'm not blaming the nurse practitioner, but I wish she had said, "Put the phone down lady, and get your butt here now!"

Skye remained alone for hours when all the doctors and nurses nervously flocked around her and debated about the best course of action. She must have been in terrible pain. She could have died then, scared, confused, and alone. I knew I would never have forgiven myself if that had happened. What did a lousy couple hours of sleep do anyway?

Somehow Skye didn't die. Over the next few days, multiple doctors from other departments came to see this medical anomaly. A warm and engaging hematologist came up from another floor and stared at Skye, mouth agape. I sensed it wasn't because she saw Skye as a freak to be ogled. I think her medical curiosity took hold. The inner nerd in me understood that a medical miracle would be too fascinating to stay away from.

The hematologist said she wanted to write a journal article about Skye's case due to her almost unbelievable sodium serum level. She theorized that the decrease in Skye's sodium levels happened slowly and meticulously. A sudden drop to such a low level would have ended in certain death.

Her opinion and general hospital practice dictated an investigation and placation of myself and Adam. Upon looking at Skye's records, the administrators discovered that Skye's serum sodium level hadn't been checked in weeks. I found it outrageous that such negligence occurred to a patient with documented low sodium levels. Up until that point, the doctors checked her sodium counts almost daily due to their unstable levels.

While Skye's history of low serum sodium levels concerned the doctors, her potassium level had reached dangerously high levels on numerous occasions. Sodium and potassium have an inverse relationship with each other. Generally, when one goes up, the other goes down. This dangerous tango coupled with Skye's initial blood serum levels meant she remained at high risk for any number of complications.

Dr. Danielpour had ordered her CBC levels taken as part of the pre-surgical wellness check. If her surgery hadn't been scheduled for Monday, the levels would have probably continued downward and caused irrevocable damage or death.

After the investigation, discussion, and consultation, the doctors came to the conclusion that the daily double tapping caused the lowered sodium counts. When the neurosurgeons tapped her brain, they took lots of fluid out, but no one thought to replace it. The level most likely crept down every day. It happened so slowly, her brain had time to adjust.

In addition, the head pediatrician felt bad about Skye's feet. Each day for months, a nurse pricked the bottom of Skye's feet to obtain a blood sample. Skye's feet had essentially become pin cushions. The head pediatrician said she stopped the daily CBC level checks so Skye's pinpricked feet could heal.

Fury overtook me. How could this group of doctors make such an incompetent mistake? A few administrators spoke to me in conference rooms about their perceived role in the situation. The head pediatrician cried and apologized because she said she only wanted Skye to have a break from the daily pokes in her feet.

I felt devastated that she hadn't consulted anyone about the decision. I would have told her to continue the daily pokes. I saw Skye's bloody, swollen feet, pin marks decorating it like a bad henna tattoo. But I also saw her CBC reports and the vacillating results. Last time I checked, other than the protagonist in Stephen King's *Pet Sematary*, no one had ever successfully raised the dead. Who cares about her feet! They would heal.

I felt even more upset that all the NICU physicians hadn't yet figured out the CSF issue. Skye couldn't possibly be the first hydrocephalic patient ever admitted to Cedars-Sinai. CSF taps weren't invented while we were inpatient. No one had connected the dots between taking fluid out of a brain and not replacing any of its components? Especially in a patient with a serious, documented history of low serum sodium counts?

Even though I wanted to pummel the doctors' faces and I felt devastated and disheartened, I instead focused my energy on Skye and her healing process. She would not be stable until the sodium levels returned to normal. Anything below normal can lead to problems.

I texted everyone and told them Skye's surgery had been postponed. I blamed some sort of general "complication" and told them I would send updates when something changed. I didn't state the facts of the situation because it wasn't anything I wanted to share. It felt too painful and raw to explain. Besides, no one would really understand.

I often end up having to take care of other people's emotions when I talk about Skye. When I share something horrible about her, the other person often reacts with fear or anxiety or asks inane questions that I can't answer. Examples: When will Skye get better? When will her vision become normal?

I reassure them that she will be okay so they stop feeling awful. Most don't realize that I barely have the spare energy to help them. I need the energy to help Skye and myself. It's usually all I can muster. I know it's hard to handle Skye's issues because I live this life.

Speaking of living the life, I had to deal with the problem at hand. The protocol for increasing Skye's sodium to a normal level would take weeks. Adam and Rowan stayed for the first few days. When they left, Skye's condition remained unstable, but the likelihood of something catastrophic happening decreased every hour. I told Adam that I felt fine and that we needed to save his time off for her shunt surgery and eventual homecoming.

I wasn't fine. But once again, I had to stick my feelings somewhere else and "woman up." I spent every day with Skye, doing my best to make sure no one else screwed up her care. Every day, her serum sodium counts rose as well as her countenance. Her chubby cheeks brightened, her breathing evened, and her cooing increased. Her brown eyes remained unseeing, but she relaxed when I stroked her hair, arms, and legs. She knew I was there.

I never allowed myself to fully relax during those three weeks. But I smiled and joked around with the nurses and other parents because Skye's sodium levels continued to head in the right direction, meaning her shunt surgery would be rescheduled. Nothing could change what had happened, and catastrophizing about it would not help Skye or me.

I called a lawyer because I wanted the hospital to pay for their mistakes. Alison, our social worker, supported us pursuing legal help, but then a few days later, she turned strangely silent. When the lawyer called back, he told me that if Skye didn't suffer lasting consequences, he couldn't pursue anything. I dropped the cause. I really didn't have a lawsuit in me at that point anyway.

After an eternity, Skye's sodium count returned to normal. The doctors removed the IV and Dr. Danielpour examined her. Pleased with the examination, he scheduled the surgery for a few days later. Dr. Danielpour reminded me that patients are usually released about forty-eight hours post-surgery. Yes! That meant we could be released as early as five or six days from that point.

I called Adam and he made arrangements to return in a few days for the surgery. I texted friends and family and told them that the surgery had been rescheduled and we *could* be home within the week. I tried to keep busy by talking to other parents and reading lowbrow celebrity magazines (one of my guiltiest habits). I felt my breaking point approaching. If anything went wrong this time, I would admit myself to the psychological ward.

Chapter Nineteen

The day of surgery arrived and all of Skye's CBC counts came back in the normal range. Attendants wheeled Skye into the operating room, and Adam, Rowan, and I went to the surgical waiting room. This room decor varies slightly at each hospital, but certain generalities exist.

In the middle of the room sit rows of uncomfortable chairs, with jutting armrests and crinkly seat covers designed to foil actual rest. Hospital brochures and out-of-date magazines lie strewn about various coffee tables, seemingly placed in no particular order. The few available outlets become a valuable commodity and families hoard them like water in a post-apocalyptic nuclear wasteland. A hospital employee sits behind a desk. They answer the phone and deal with family members' questions and concerns.

Like a stock market ticker, a large computer screen lists each patient's medical ID number (for privacy) and the patient's status. Families see that the patient has entered the operating room, is in active surgery, or is in recovery. I always love watching Skye move through the process. I feel some semblance of control.

A shunt surgery usually lasts forty-five minutes so we weren't waiting long before her status changed from "in surgery" to "in recovery." While it was no guarantee, at least we knew Skye wasn't bleeding out on the operating table.

Once Skye moved to "in recovery," a hospital employee called our name and sent us up to the NICU. Adam and I breathed normally for the first time that day. He headed upstairs to see Skye and I played with Rowan. After he texted me that she remained stable in the NICU, Rowan and I headed to Ronald McDonald House. I desperately wanted to see Skye, but since kids under twelve aren't allowed in the NICU, one of us had to stay with Rowan.

I felt giddy. I looked around the RMH room and fantasized about sweeping our remaining belongings into a bag and heading home. I knew that in two days, the fantasy would become reality. We would drive home together. Rowan would play with his own toys and I would sleep in my own bed. I would cook with my own pots and pans. I thought about the restaurants I wanted to visit, and which friends I would call first.

Adam came back to RMH that night. He said that Skye mainly slept and that the only sign of the surgery was a heart-shaped bandage on the top of her head. The nurses seemed pleased with her vital signs and the doctors would come by the next morning during rounds to discuss things further. I slept soundly.

The next morning, I went to the NICU. Skye looked peaceful and slept off and on. The doctor and the discharge nurse started rounds. I anxiously awaited our turn. The doctor looked at Skye and examined her bandage and vital signs. He made a few cursory comments and left. The discharge nurse stayed with me and smiled. She brought out a large file with Skye's name on the label.

She took a paper from the file and showed it to me. The top of the paper stated Skye's discharge date. For a second, my heart stopped. The paper listed the discharge date as two weeks out. I did some mental math to make sure I wasn't crazy. I looked at the paper again. I hadn't misread the date.

"I don't understand the date…" I trailed off and couldn't speak.

"I know Dr. Danielpour said she would be discharged forty-eight hours post-surgery, but the doctors decided to keep her here for two more weeks to monitor her serum sodium levels. If the levels stay stable for the two weeks, she can leave then."

Something broke in my brain. Staying in the NICU for two more weeks sounded like a prison sentence. My heart caught on fire. I dropped to my knees and moaned. The discharge nurse tried to comfort me but all I heard was blah, blah, blah. I didn't move and my moans became louder.

The discharge nurse went and called Alison, our social worker. Alison helped me stand up and walked me to a conference room. I slumped down on a couch. I don't remember anything she said. I just kept repeating, "I can't do it, I can't do it, I can't do it."

I'm sure Alison validated my feelings and offered empathetic comments. That's what I do when one of my clients insists they can't bear an impending situation. How much easier it is on the other end!

Eventually I stopped my maddening assertions and breathed. I wiped my tears away and stood up. I called Adam and let him know what was going on. He gasped and sighed, but his reaction was annoyingly typical. I wanted him to rage and cry and scream about the indignation. Instead, he planned the trip back home and casually accepted the doctor's decision.

Adam and Rowan left the next day and I faced the dreadful weeks. I felt terrified we would never leave. Adam didn't understand that if Skye's sodium levels fell, or if she exhibited a fever or symptoms of a cold, we would not leave in two weeks. At any time, the date could be pushed back.

He didn't have to live the NICU life every day. He slept in his own bed, went to work with known colleagues, saw his friends, and socialized. He slept through every night. He didn't have excess weight to lose. He didn't have to express milk every three hours like a dairy cow.

In retrospect, I know he experienced his own private hell. He took care of Rowan, worked a stressful full-time job, and drove to and from L.A. most weekends. Even though he wasn't living the NICU day in and out, he had a sick daughter with an uncertain future. He worried about my mental state and anxiety level. He probably felt helpless.

I called my friend Lisa and cried and whined about the unfairness of staying longer. I felt crushed and defeated. My steel trap of a mind was rusting and failing. The raging bear was almost loose. Lisa demonstrated her dedication to me by hanging up the phone, getting in her car, and driving four hours to L.A.

I cannot overstate what that meant to me. Months before, when Skye was only a week old, my aunt Betsy flew out from Ohio to see us. I will not forget her generosity. She spent money that she didn't have on a plane ticket and hotel so she could support me. Another friend happened to be in L.A shortly after Skye's birth and she and her husband met me for coffee. Adam's parents visited right after Skye's birth.

I did not expect my other friends and family to fly three thousand miles or drive four hours to see me. I hoped that more of them would do so, but I never asked. I don't think most of them realized the pain and suffering that I experienced. Maybe some of them didn't want to deal with seeing Skye. Most likely everyone else felt that they were too busy to make it down. I don't harbor negative feelings about anyone, but in hindsight, I wish more of our friends had made the effort to visit us.

When Lisa came to visit, she spent the night with me in RMH (shh, don't tell). We talked about our friends and the weather and her kids. I didn't want to talk about Skye and myself. Her visit allowed me a sense of desperately needed normalcy. I craved the banal and ordinary. I had suffered enough chaos and uncertainty to last a lifetime.

To use a running metaphor, it isn't the first mile of a marathon that seems impossible. I had rounded the bend of mile eighteen and I felt ready to drop out of the race. Lisa became my cheering sideline fan with a cup of water and a gel pack of nutrients. I still had to run the last 8.2 miles, but she supported me the whole way.

After Lisa left, I knew it was up to me to finish strong. I felt exhausted and isolated and terrified. But no one else could take the burden for me. Even though I felt like the time would never end, I knew rationally that we would leave the hospital at some point.

Chapter Twenty

I called my friend Hannah who had a six-year-old daughter with special needs.

"When we get home, what do I do?" I asked.

I knew her daughter attended various therapies and received services, but I had no idea where to begin. In true Hannah style, she sent me a detailed email with information about obtaining services for Skye. It listed the phone numbers and agencies I needed to contact.

I read and re-read her email. A daunting task lay ahead. With Rowan, it had seemed difficult enough sorting out doctor visits, vaccinations, daycare options, and food choices. How ignorant I was! I had lived blissfully unaware of the subculture of parents who have children with special needs.

I didn't understand how different their lives might be from mine. All parents are inherently more alike than different. Yet parents who have children with special needs navigate a strange, unique existence.

Hannah's email explained services like early intervention, speech therapy, vision services, supplemental insurance, and behavior services. Each one of these required separate assessments, appointments, and medical records. Every step required filling out endless forms.

As I read the email, I felt like my life no longer belonged to me.

My choices and potential career began fading away into nothing. How could I ever work again? Would my graduate degree sit on the shelf, a glorified paperweight? Skye seemed like she would need every service. How would I begin sorting through it all?

I remembered Anne Lamont's wonderful anecdote in *Bird by Bird: Some Instructions on Writing and Life* about her brother writing a school essay on birds. He had put off the assignment for weeks and finally sat down the night before the due date. As he sat exasperated at the table, his wise father sat down beside him and offered counsel: "Bird by bird, buddy. Just take it bird by bird."

I picked up the phone and called my local Regional Center, a California state-run nonprofit that provides services to children and adults with disabilities. From birth to age three, Regional Center provides free in-home services like speech therapy, early-start intervention therapy, case management, and behavior services.

Once a child turns three, a team conducts an assessment to see if the child still qualifies for services. If they do qualify, Regional Center continues funding services for the child and they enter a special class in the local school district.

Less affected children, especially those with an unclear diagnosis, sometimes get dropped from Regional Center at the age of three. In a way, it's good to hear that someone had been cut off. That means the child isn't severely affected by their disabilities. However, it also becomes harder to obtain services for the family.

> **Spoiler Alert:** Skye is a slam dunk and qualifies for pretty much all services.

I talked to the Regional Center representative. I answered questions about Skye's estimated functioning abilities and probable discharge date. I made a tentative appointment with them for an initial assessment, assuming we would be home by then.

Once I hung up the phone, my inner efficiency expert kicked in. I spent the next few weeks talking to insurance representatives in order to get pre-approved for appointments with medical specialists. I talked to our pediatrician's office and started the referral process to local agencies and doctors. I made scattered appointments for assessments and initial exams.

At that point, Skye had been receiving physical therapy and occupational therapy in the NICU. Physical therapy (PT) deals with gross motor tasks: walking, legs, ankles, and feet. Occupational therapy (OT) focuses on fine motor tasks: reaching, hands, arms, and shoulders. In the NICU setting, during both OT and PT, therapists stretched Skye's arms and legs and set up stimulating toys in her crib. All the toys made some sort of noise so she could attempt to locate them.

Skye's right arm seemed less capable than her left, but overall it didn't seem too bad. She seemed stiff, but all four appendages straightened out. Skye's physical therapist told me that since Skye was young, no one could predict what her limbs might look like in the future. I learned my first of many lessons about the variability of cerebral palsy.

Growth spurts are not a friend of the child with cerebral palsy. Muscles are often already tight and stretched. When the child grows, the taut muscles struggle to keep up with an already taxing change for anyone's body. Sometimes joints will tighten and contract during this time, increasing pain, and decreasing mobility.

Even though Skye had a diagnosis of cerebral palsy (CP), I didn't understand much about how it would affect her. I felt disappointed that she already had a major problem, especially an incurable one. But I had many other known issues to contend with. CP didn't feel like the primary concern.

Skye lay on her back, head tilted slightly to the left. She moved her limbs, although not much. I still thought she was blind. Every so often she would show interest in a toy if it were placed in her hand. She had a grasping reflex and ate fairly well.

I worried about her having a shunt malfunction. I didn't know if we could ever go on a plane or camp or travel abroad. I didn't understand yet that I had to deeply compartmentalize the shunt. A person cannot live life worrying about something that might happen.

Most babies don't have much personality during the first few months of life. Skye had even less of one. Her muted affect and seemingly nonexistent eyesight clouded my ability to form a solid attachment with her. I eventually learned to love her ferociously, but it wasn't happening yet. Uncertainty and fear still held sway over my love for her at that point.

I can't remember how I filled the gaps of time any more than a person can relate every minute of every hour spent on a long drive. One day during those last maddening weeks, I visited Skye as usual. Her physical therapist stopped by and asked a few questions about Skye's behavior. She had recently read about a visual issue called cortical visual impairment (CVI). She didn't know much about the impairment, but she thought it sounded a bit like Skye. It would be worth looking into.

I went out to the waiting room and searched for CVI on my phone. I opened the first article I saw. Caused by a brain injury, CVI consists of ten characteristic behaviors. Patients generally have normal ocular structures. However, the brain structures associated with vision - visual neural pathways and occipital lobes - behave improperly.

I knew immediately that Skye had CVI. I felt both completely validated ("I was right!") and irritated ("How could they miss this?") with the hospital doctors. I couldn't believe they hadn't heard about it since they dealt with so many cases of brain damage and brain bleeds in the NICU.

Even though receiving a diagnosis can feel stressful and sad, it's infinitely better to know the exact nature of the problem. With a diagnosis, families can obtain services and therapies that can help optimize the child's happiness and functioning. Classmates, friends, and family members better understand the reasons behind certain behaviors and challenges. Support groups exist for families who have kids with the same diagnosis.

Some parents don't want to stigmatize their child by placing a diagnosis in their permanent record. They worry their child won't get into the military, or get a job with the government or at a school. Maybe insurance will consider it a pre-existing condition and discriminate against them in the future. Those scenarios are possible.

If a child is functioning fairly well, this strategy might work out. I know plenty of adults with families and great jobs who are obviously on the spectrum (they have autism, whether they received an official diagnosis or not).

However, I don't have the luxury of choosing whether to accept a diagnosis, so I don't feel too sorry for their dilemma. If their worst problem is vacillating between getting that autism diagnosis or not, then their kid can't be too bad. If he were severe, they wouldn't have a choice.

I made an appointment for Skye to see a pediatric ophthalmologist once we returned home. CVI is unique because it's a visual impairment that can actually improve over time. The articles indicated that it was a brain injury with neuroplastic potential, so I felt hopeful. Even though her "blindness" didn't bother me as much as I thought it might, I still didn't like it!

Our departure day (the day of the blue buggy!) finally arrived. The nurse reviewed the endless paperwork and discharge instructions. Skye's vital signs were excellent, and her sodium serum count was normal. I skimmed and signed as fast as I could.

All of us NICU veterans had heard stories about babies ready to leave in the blue buggy. According to legend, right as the mother began to walk out, a nurse noticed the baby looked flush. Lo and behold, the baby had a low-grade fever and had to stay another day (or more).

My feet felt like lead and my stomach felt on fire. I noticed the discharge nurse had three pens sticking out of her pocket. Her shirt sat slightly askew. She moved like molasses as she read every line aloud and triple-checked every box and signature line. I knew she had to complete everything, but I wanted to knock her head off and run.

Once the discharge nurse finally declared us checked out, I hugged her. I wheeled Skye's blue buggy out of the room and walked briskly but cautiously. As we walked through the hallway and into the lobby, I hugged the nurses and the moms and the fellows and the doctors. Some were crying. Not me. I had a smile from ear to ear.

Chapter Twenty-One

Somehow I survived my time in the NICU. I know I have lingering post-traumatic stress disorder symptoms from my experience there. It's not the same experience that a soldier faces in combat, but in its own way, the NICU is a type of battlefield.

The time I spent there traumatized me, and even though I've done EMDR (a technique for reducing trauma symptoms) and talk therapy, I still cry when I remember myself living in that room for so many weeks.

Recently, another mom and I spoke at a party, and she discussed her NICU stay much more casually. I couldn't believe it wasn't a major stressor for her. But then we discussed a few differences and I understood.

Her son was born prematurely, a routine issue for our local NICU. She stayed in her own home with her husband while I stayed at RMH with domestic violence on the other side of my wall. She ate her usual meals while I lived on Wendy's value meals. She slept in her own bed, socialized with friends, and shopped at familiar grocery stores. I slept on a stained mattress, had no friends, and shopped at grocery stores that offered suspiciously colored meats and strange candy.

The other mom just couldn't relate. Fluid bubbles popping up from Skye's skull? Needles inserted into her head twice a day? A near-death experience at three months old? We were playing a different sport.

I don't remember everything I said or did or thought in the NICU. Some memories are lost. Some memories rush back at unexpected times. I remember the main nurses who worked with Skye, a few moms, and some of the babies. Everything else is blocked off somewhere.

If I kept it all fresh and available, I wouldn't get up in the morning. I know I have some pretty heavy duty defense mechanisms in place. As a mental health therapist, I know these are unhealthy, but they also help me get through the day.

When a situation becomes too intense, I can dissociate and disappear into myself until I can handle what is being presented to me. I intellectualize to help convince myself that everything will end up working out (even though it really might not). I can also utilize compartmentalization, in which I put aside all of my terrible feelings and fears that I don't have time to deal with.

I can't replace the defense mechanisms with healthy coping skills because I have to survive each day. I don't have the time or energy to walk around in a mindful state of bliss while chewing bark and chanting "om." Skye and I eventually left the NICU, but my special needs journey had just begun.

For the first few months at home, we lived in a strange limbo of uncertainty and happiness. Skye smiled and began subtle interactions with others. Even though her motor movements seemed slow, she could move all four limbs. She lay on her back. Hair grew over her shunt but it still bulged out. We kept hats on her most of the time. To a casual observer, she could pass for a typical baby.

Skye's personality emerged and we were delighted to see her developing joy and humor. She was not a vegetable! She didn't see well but she could hear and feel. We played music and placed toys in her hands. We talked to her about the day and the weather. Rowan showed Skye his various toy trucks and cars, explaining what each one was and how they were different from each other.

Our family and friends could scarcely understand what sort of baby we brought home. They visited and tenderly touched Skye and asked questions that we couldn't answer, like when she would talk and how well she would see. Even though Skye did well in many regards, the statistics were not in her favor. She had suffered a severe brain injury. Undoubtedly, she would suffer negative consequences. Everyone wanted to hear about a happy ending. I shrugged.

We visited follow-up doctors. A pediatric ophthalmologist confirmed the diagnosis of cortical visual impairment (CVI). The doctor also diagnosed Skye with optic nerve dysplasia. Her optic nerves had been damaged by the stroke, affecting her visual acuity.

As of today, there is nothing we can do about her optic nerve dysplasia. However, we could do something about her CVI. We could use the concept of neuroplasticity to re-train Skye's brain. After researching CVI, I found the best and most consistent resource to be Christine Roman-Lantzy. She studied and worked with patients who had a CVI diagnosis. She wrote a manual about retraining the damaged brain called *Cortical Visual Impairment: An Approach to Assessment and Intervention.*

The book describes three phases of CVI simply titled I, II, and III. Roman-Lantzy provides dozens of ways to progress a child through each stage. She based her information and techniques on evidence-based science.

Excitement and purpose filled me up again. I read her book, highlighting relevant passages and dog-earing important pages.

I observed Skye and completed assessments to establish baseline data. Skye's baseline tested low, so she sat squarely in phase I. The crux of phase I involved using bright colors, movement, and sound to elicit any use of vision. Skye probably wouldn't see details or attend to any visual stimuli for long periods. Rather, Skye needed to understand that she had visual capability.

No matter the amount of brain training and time, Skye will never have normal vision. A visual impairment is at its core a permanent condition. However, a person with CVI can obtain *functional* vision. By working through the phases, a person with CVI can eventually see outlines of figures and shapes, understand color, and differentiate between objects. By setting up specific environmental cues for Skye, we allowed her brain the opportunity to rewire so vision could incrementally return.

Imagine looking through a piece of swiss cheese. This is similar to how a person with CVI might see. Cluttered backgrounds or busy-looking pictures are nearly impossible to decipher. Books or other stimuli should have simple pictures, large font, and bold, bright colors. Movement, texture, lights, and 3-D objects are best, especially at first.

After assessing Skye, I noticed that she preferred yellow and red colors. We bought yellow and red plates, forks, and cups. During feeding times, we tapped her plate to indicate its location. We tapped until she found the spoon or the bite of food.

I bought yellow and red mylar balloons and a red lava lamp. I put the lamp in front of a large black foam board to block out all other stimuli. I turned on the lamp and encouraged Skye to watch it as the red oil clumped and moved.

Skye made wonderful gains during this time. While lying on her back one day, she began looking at the whirling blades of the ceiling fan above her. Woohoo! Skye probably wasn't "seeing" the ceiling fan, but she noticed the movement. Finally, she looked at something with purpose!

She started batting at toys, reaching out for objects if they moved or made noise, and moving her head to see objects or people. Skye completed phase I and began working on phase II goals. I showed her more colors, more meaningful materials, and incrementally more complicated visual stimuli. For example, I placed a blue spoon by her red plate. Or we read her a book with smaller pictures. I almost couldn't believe how much visual progress she made in a few months.

Chapter Twenty-Two

Like a beachcomber collecting shells, we collected disabilities and services during those months. A Regional Center case manager and occupational therapist came to our house to assess Skye for services.

"What does she do for fun?" they asked.

"Looks at lava lamps," I said.

"What's her medical history?"

"I think you're going to need a bigger notebook."

They observed Skye throughout the assessment and asked me to play with her. Because she tested at a lower percentile than her typically developing peers, Skye qualified for services through the Regional Center.

I both welcomed and resented the in-home services. It is arguably easier for therapists to come to me than it is driving to an agency. However, I could never shake the feeling that county workers might judge the dirty floor my child lies on. I turned into my grandmother and scoured the pots and pans before the guests arrived.

From the ages of 0-3, Regional Center covered Skye's in-home services. Early intervention is the key to saving resources and money in the long run. Because of neuroplasticity, the child's brain is like a sponge. The first five years of life are the best time to teach skills, increase listening comprehension, and learn languages. Any time and energy put into a child during those first few years will help the child for the rest of their life.

In addition to Regional Center, California Children's Services (CCS) evaluated Skye and determined she was eligible for physical therapy and occupational therapy. Both therapies take place at an agency site in the county. Every six months, CCS completes an evaluation to determine service eligibility.

Fun Fact: Skye is the grand champion of qualifying for services.

We also made an appointment to see a pediatric neurologist, Dr. Balke. Only one pediatric neurologist serves our area, but luckily, she says things like, "If it were my daughter, I would..." She doesn't sugarcoat the facts, but she takes time to consider options and possibilities. If she doesn't know the answer, she says so, and recommends someone who might know.

We first met Dr. Balke when Skye was five months old. Like most people who read Skye's chart before meeting her, Dr. Balke expressed surprise when we entered the room. Skye's brain damage looks horrific on paper. Dr. Balke examined Skye's head and legs and arms. She asked me questions about the NICU stay and the reason they put her on and, subsequently, took her off phenobarbital.

She asked me about Skye's basic skills and her eyesight. She knew about CVI and said it made perfect sense that Skye would exhibit its classic characteristics. Because we live in a less populated area, Dr. Balke knew almost everyone involved in Skye's care personally.

Even though Dr. Balke said she had no idea what Skye would be like when she was twenty, I left the appointment in a good mental space. With such a fabulous doctor on our team, I felt more optimistic.

I began wrapping my head around the concept that I had a child with special needs. At that point in time, we had four diagnoses and counting: cerebral palsy, nystagmus, cortical visual impairment, and optic nerve dysplasia. I had a child with multiple disabilities. Holy crap.

I began to develop a system of categorization: orthopedic (motor functions), speech, social, cognitive, and vision. I found that Skye would expand in one or two areas while other systems seemed stagnant. Then, sometimes, when I needed it most, she would suddenly advance in another area. All of the systems remained fluid throughout. Orthopedic issues became more pronounced with time, and speech seemed lost until she reached almost five years old.

Over time I became a surrogate physical therapist, occupational therapist, speech therapist, doctor, neurologist, radiologist, and teacher. I had to become an expert in order to advocate for my daughter.

Chapter Twenty-Three

One day when Skye was six months old, we visited a friend who lived on the third floor of an apartment building. While we rode in the elevator, Skye's eyes flickered up and she seemingly threw her hands in the air. I looked closely at her but she looked fine. Adam and Rowan stood in front of me so they didn't see anything.

Throughout the next few hours, she did the same thing again about four times. I pulled Adam to the side and told him what I had seen. He wasn't worried because Skye often behaved abnormally. But I knew with absolute certainty that something was wrong.

I didn't think she had a seizure. I had only seen one person have a seizure and it was a tonic-clonic seizure - the kind you see in movies where the person falls down, jerking and foaming at the mouth.

I looked online but couldn't find anything that fit her specific behaviors. Confused, I made a mental note to mention it the next time we saw her primary physician. I watched her like a hawk for the rest of the day and saw nothing more.

A few days later, Adam played with Skye in our bedroom, tickling her belly and feet. I folded laundry in our living room while Rowan played with some blocks and toy cars on the floor beside me.

"Come in here quick!" Adam yelled.

I ran into the room. Adam looked freaked out. Skye was throwing her arms up in the air over and over. Her eyes rolled back in her head. I grabbed my phone and dialed 911. I told them she was having a seizure because I didn't know what else to say.

The firefighters arrived first. Even though they came quickly, Skye had stopped her movements by the time they arrived. I sat in shock. I clutched Skye's hand and peered into her eyes. A firefighter told me to move out of the way and started examining her.

One of the firefighters played Hot Wheels with Rowan in the living room. How cool is that? Rowan didn't blink an eye amid the chaos. I guess he didn't know any better.

The paramedics arrived shortly after. Adam and I tried not to panic. The paramedics took Skye's pulse and vital signs. She checked out fine. They stayed awhile to observe and ask us questions, but she didn't have any more movements. Her eyes had returned to baseline. All the medical personnel left and told us to call our neurologist the next day.

After everyone left, I saw the half-folded laundry askew in its basket. It didn't seem like mine. Nothing in the room seemed like mine anymore. Rowan continued to play as if the strange cacophony of men hadn't just entered and left. A neighbor knocked on our door and asked if we were okay.

"The whole neighborhood saw the sirens," she said. "We all assumed it was your daughter."

I told her we weren't sure what was going on, but we appreciated her concern. Sirens are big news in a small town. It was probably the most interesting incident the neighborhood experienced that month.

We called Dr. Balke's office the next morning and made an appointment for the following week. While we waited, Skye seemed completely fine. She smiled, played, and continued to breastfeed.

But every few days, she would have short bursts of the same movements: throwing her arms up and rolling her eyes back.

Sometimes her eyes watered. We weren't sure what to think so we just took it day by day.

I took Skye to the appointment with Dr. Balke. She asked me questions about what the movements looked like. She asked if I had a video, which I did not. From then on, I took a short video of any suspicious events.

Dr. Balke then gave me some advice, which I have followed for years, and passed on to others. She advised me to keep these types of videos short; no doctor wants to sit down and watch someone else's daughter eat lunch for ten minutes, waiting to see a possible seizure. I should get to the point quickly.

Dr. Balke left the room to grab her computer so she could look up possible explanations. In a stroke of extraordinary "luck," Skye began having the movements right then. This never happens! It's like hearing a weird grinding noise in your car. When you take it into the shop, the mechanic starts up what sounds like a perfectly good engine. Nobody ever has a seizure or a headache or pain during the doctor's visit. It always happens in the parking lot on the way out.

I ran into the hallway and found Dr. Balke.

"She's having the movements," I said.

She grabbed her computer and followed me back to the room. She watched Skye for a few moments. After the movements seemed done, Skye sucked her thumb and acted as if nothing happened.

Dr. Balke looked at me and said, "I think she might have infantile spasms."

I didn't know anything about this term yet, so it meant nothing to me. "Infantile spasms" even sounded mild. However, Dr. Balke's face looked quite serious and a bit sad. She sighed and asked me some questions about our insurance coverage. I thought it was quite good, but I didn't know much about specifics.

She explained that infantile spasms are a type of seizure that usually occur as a result of brain damage. Skye's brain injury made her a perfect candidate for having seizures so she wasn't surprised.

"I don't want you to run home and research this because it will look terrible. We don't know anything for sure until we do an EEG. We can do a brief one locally and get an idea of what we're dealing with."

Dr. Balke repeated her warnings against me researching online, but I secretly knew (and I'm sure she did too) that I would be doing exactly that when I returned home.

I knew the definition of an EEG (electroencephalogram) from a college class, but I never had any direct experience. An EEG measures brain waves in order to ascertain abnormalities, including seizure activity. They aren't always accurate. Sometimes the EEG misses issues deep in the brain, and sometimes the EEG shows abnormalities but the person doesn't exhibit seizures. Also, a person has to have a seizure while hooked up to the EEG machine. Otherwise, the doctors can't definitively diagnose.

Infantile spasms are fairly easy to diagnose because of a distinct, abnormal EEG pattern that is usually present in conjunction with stereotyped physical actions. These consist of aimless, repetitive motor movements like throwing one's arms in the air, rocking, or thumb sucking.

Dr. Balke asked her secretary to schedule an EEG at our local hospital as soon as possible. We scheduled a follow-up appointment with her so we could discuss the results of the EEG and make a plan of action depending on what it showed. I asked some basic questions but didn't really know what answers I needed.

Once we returned home, I turned on my computer. In theory, Dr. Balke was right about not researching, but I needed to know what we might be dealing with. I typed "infantile spasms" in the search bar and braced myself.

It was worse than I imagined. Every article and website began with a paragraph detailing the "unfortunate children and their families" who deal with such a "catastrophic" and "devastating" type of epilepsy. Almost all children who have infantile spasms are developmentally delayed later in life. Many of them are globally delayed.

I read lots of articles. Then I looked at articles cited by *those* articles and read more. No matter how much I read, it was all the same. Children with significant brain damage are at risk of developing infantile spasms. Some seemingly typical children develop them as well. Those children are the ones who most likely grow out of it by age four or five.

Children with brain damage tend to fare the worst. Twenty percent of them develop Lennoux Gestault Syndrome - a really bad type of epilepsy. Some children with brain damage might grow out of infantile spasms but will later develop other types of epilepsy, like drop seizures (very nasty), complex partial seizures, or tonic-clonic seizures.

The articles described infantile spasms as "terrible and catastrophic" because they cause *constant* abnormal brain waves, equaling hundreds of seizures each day. Children lose skills as development slows down. Their hijacked brains can't keep up with critical brain growth.

I felt the joy seep out of my bones. My child would suffer and I didn't know what to do.

Chapter Twenty-Four

I love weather. I grew up in Ohio where extreme weather is a fact of life. In Ohio they say, "If you want the weather to change, just wait five minutes." However, I hated experiencing freezing temperatures in winter. Nobody likes ice except penguins.

Even though I avoid the ice by living in California, I do miss one aspect of Midwestern weather: summer thunderstorms. I can still picture the pounding rain, a purple and black horizon, huge, saturated clouds sweeping overhead, lightning crackling and sizzling, thunder booming and roaring. I remember lying in my bed and listening to the torrents of rain, watching my window shake from the wind and thunder, and witnessing dozens of vicious lightning strikes. Thunderstorms were a highlight of my childhood. It gave me great comfort to snuggle in my bed, warm and safe beneath my blankets, while the wild storm raged and howled outside.

Seizures are like electrical storms. When a lightning bolt strikes a tree, the intense electricity obliterates whatever parts of the tree it touches, leaving smoking, black remnants on its branches and trunk. Likewise, a seizure consists of major electrical pulses surging through brain neurons. Short and isolated seizures won't necessarily damage the neurons, but severe, long-term seizures most certainly will. Neither the tree nor the neurons will ever fully recover from such horrific electrical attacks. I don't think anyone has ever been struck by lightning and said, "Gee that felt great! I'll have another."

Most seizures consist of three phases: promodal, active seizure, and postictal. During the prodromal phase, a person might have hours of strange feelings, visions, sounds, or thoughts. This can help some people get to a safe place before a seizure hits. They might have time to tell their parents, or start some deep breathing and meditation.

During the active phase of the seizure, people twitch or jerk or fall or stare into space or drop to the ground. Sometimes people lose consciousness and sometimes they don't. People usually don't die from having an active seizure itself. They die from falling over and hitting their head on the bathtub or driving their car into a guardrail or drowning in a pool. People are discouraged from showering alone if they have seizures, although I don't know if anyone actually follows that advice.

During the postictal phase, the active seizure ends and the body recovers. This can take hours or days. Sometimes a person sleeps or becomes irritable. Sometimes a person seems fine. Skye seemed a bit tired after her spasms, but not too noticeable at first.

On the day of the EEG, Adam and I took Skye to our local hospital and checked in. Since it's a small hospital compared to Cedars-Sinai, the admitting department processed our paperwork rather quickly. But, the local hospital doesn't have an epilepsy department. Dr. Balke is the outside doctor who reads the results of every EEG done there.

Two EEG technicians helped prepare Skye's head for the electrograph. They placed twenty-four electrodes on her scalp with strong adhesive. For the uninitiated, this stuff is superglue on steroids. Obviously, it does not easily wash out of hair. Placing electrodes is a long, tedious process. The electrodes have to be placed on an exact spot on the scalp and pressed down with glue until they stick.

Skye fussed and cried and wailed the whole time. It didn't look painful but it did look extremely uncomfortable. It took more time to set up the test than to actually run the test. Once the technicians positioned all the electrodes, Skye lay on her back for twenty minutes. Her brainwaves showed on a computer screen. I had no idea what to look for.

EEGs are complicated so it takes a specially trained person to read them. Every time Skye moved, the EEG showed a blip. These blips are technically called artifacts, designating false abnormalities. Skye lay fairly still but she moved her arms and legs. It was Dr. Balke's job to interpret the brainwaves while recognizing and ignoring the artifacts.

Once the technicians removed the electrodes, we scrubbed Skye's head with hot water and towels. We left the hospital and waited at home. The hospital sent Dr. Balke a disc with Skye's EEG brainwaves. We didn't talk about it with anyone else because we didn't have enough information ourselves.

I sat on pins and needles all day, pacing and staring off into space. I lay awake all night thinking about every horrible outcome.

A few days later, Dr. Balke viewed the disc. She called and said she would squeeze us in the next day for an appointment. That told me almost everything I needed to know. This probably wouldn't be good.

The next day, Dr. Balke delivered the news that Skye did indeed have infantile spasms. Dr. Balke said she had other patients with spasms and some did better than others. Some responded to medication and some didn't. Some suffered severe cognitive delays and some didn't. I sat while she spoke, hands clenched, looking at Skye. A nurse laughed in the background and it seemed so discordant. Didn't she realize the world was ending?

I still had hope that Skye would somehow end up okay. I wasn't in denial about the diagnosis, but I was in denial about the *severity* of her disabilities. While Rowan (still only two years old!) played at our feet, Dr. Balke told Adam and me about the standard treatments for infantile spasms.

The first line of treatment is usually medication. Some doctors recommend trying a ketogenic diet first. But Dr. Balke didn't recommend this due to its strictness and low compliance rates over time.

Despite Dr. Balke's expertise, this diagnosis meant we now needed to see a pediatric epileptologist, a neurologist who specializes in children with epilepsy. Dr. Balke recommended Dr. Sankar at UCLA, with its renowned epilepsy department. Since the necessary referral forms and insurance approvals would take time to process, we called our insurance company that day to make sure Dr. Sankar and any tests or procedures would be covered and to obtain pre-approval.

Fun Fact: There are no fun facts about calling insurance companies.

Dr. Balke also prescribed Zonegran, an anti-seizure medication. The seizures essentially hijacked Skye's brain. Most of her energy went to surviving the attack. It didn't leave much time for playing and learning new skills, using her imagination, or moving her body. Some kids grow out of the spasms by age four or five, but that would be too much crucial time lost! We were in a race for her cognition.

We filled the prescription for Zonegran that same day. I started charting the attacks, hoping that the seizures would stop after a few days on the medication. I felt sure Zonegran would work. I was a seizure newbie - totally ignorant and not yet bitter and jaded.

After a week on Zonegran, Skye developed a rash on her arm. It grew bigger each day, so Dr. Balke told us to stop the medication. It hadn't made a difference anyway. Disappointment washed over me.

I felt so desperate to help Skye that I put all my hope and faith into a tiny blue pill. I didn't have personal experience taking prescription drugs, and I had never dealt with the trial and error process usually involved with finding the right fit.

Next we tried a medication called Sabril. It can have really nasty side effects like severe sleepiness and irritability. It also has horrific risks, including permanent vision loss. It seemed crazy, but we needed the big guns to shut the seizures down. We couldn't sit around waiting until someone at UCLA decided to meet us and make a plan. We had to try something.

Some prescription medications can be filled the same day. Antibiotics, certain anti-seizure drugs, antidepressants, and anti-anxiety medications are usually stocked on-site at pharmacies. But some medications require insurance pre-approval. Maybe the medication has scary side effects or is being used off-label and needs medical justification. Since Sabril had such scary side effects, it required pre-approval. Dr. Balke's secretary worked on getting the approval from our insurance company.

Meanwhile, Dr. Balke told us about a case of infantile spasms cured by a local homeopath. Homeopathy is an alternative approach to medicine involving holistic and natural cures. Homeopaths use remedies such as plants and minerals. Dr. Balke said she doubted homeopathy's effectiveness, but since we had to wait for Sabril, it wouldn't hurt to try.

Chapter Twenty-Five

The homeopathic doctor smiled and seemed genuinely concerned with helping us. Skye sat in her baby carrier next to my feet while I explained our issue. Skye had a cluster of spasms while we spoke and the homeopath watched her.

"That doesn't seem too bad," he said. "Pretty mild seizures."

Already annoyed with his lack of knowledge, I mumbled something about it being really bad and needing help. He asked a lot of questions and consulted his homeopathic guidebooks. The guidebooks provide information about dozens of remedies for various ailments.

He prescribed a remedy and gave us an envelope with its powdery substance inside. We gave Skye half its contents there in his office. He instructed me to give her the other half the next day. After observing her for about five days, I would call him back to see if it worked. If not, he had a few other ideas.

After five days, I called him and said we saw no change. We went in one more time and he gave us a second remedy. It was the same instruction and a similar powder, but with a different ingredient. We again saw no change so I called and let him know the results. He sounded surprised that it hadn't worked.

Even though I doubted the remedies would work, I felt disheartened anyway. Part of me wanted to believe so badly. I let my guard down and it hurt my soul. I felt insanely jealous of the other family whose child took a powder remedy and never had seizures again. Why not us too? What had my daughter done to deserve such a fate? I had done some unsavory things in my life. Maybe I deserved some negative karma. But not Skye. Not an innocent baby.

We could only proceed so far with the homeopathic treatment. Remedies aren't cheap. Insurance doesn't cover homeopathic treatment because it isn't evidence-based. Sufficient valid research studies haven't proven that homeopathic treatments work.

Of course, it's possible homeopathy doesn't work at all. However, it's also possible that homeopathy does work. Maybe more studies should be undertaken. Maybe the completed studies contain flaws and problems.

In order for definitive change, researchers must conduct lots of double-blind long-term studies. Neither the participants nor the people administering the treatment can know the expected outcome. Everyone remains "blind" to what the experimenters are looking for, which should decrease bias.

Essential oils are another treatment without evidence-based research. Insurance doesn't cover treatment with essential oils nor will most medical doctors recommend their use. Once again, people who use essential oils aren't necessarily quacks. In order to be taken seriously, double-blind studies proving their worthiness must be published in esteemed medical journals.

During conferences, rehabilitation stints, and in hospital waiting rooms, many people have approached me about using essential oils on Skye. Several of my friends sell essential oils. Because of them, I own an essential oil diffuser and multiple oils. A friend made me an anxiety mix which I rub on my wrists. I don't know if it helps but it hasn't increased my anxiety at least.

Some people feel essential oils can cure anything. I remain

skeptical of anyone who feels only one answer exists to a complicated problem. If it were that simple, we would all be rubbing oil of oregano and frankincense on ourselves every day.

Someone told me to rub lavender essential oil on Skye's feet every night and it would cure her seizures and cerebral palsy. I think diffusing lavender is heavenly. It certainly hides the smell of poop and vomit. However, there isn't a cure for cerebral palsy any more than there is a cure for having brown hair.

It's dangerous to use essential oils without proper research and guidance. Every time I went to a hospital or rehabilitation center with Skye, I met moms who sold and/or used essential oils. Some were well-versed and smart and didn't push. They had attended workshops and read books on how to use oils safely. I listened and tried samples that they found useful for their child.

I tried essential oils because I couldn't just rely on evidence-based methods. I was a desperate mother. One child's infantile spasms were cured by a homeopathic doctor. That means it might help someone else. And why not us? Skye's issues were so complicated that even the best medical doctors in the world couldn't always help us. For me, it was paramount to try almost anything.

Unfortunately, we came to the conclusion that homeopathy wasn't helping Skye. I felt a deep well of disappointment. I put faith in his methods because I wanted to believe it could work. Even though one avenue had been closed, I felt determined to find another way to stop her seizures.

Chapter Twenty-Six

Shortly after we ended our relationship with the homeopathic doctor, the insurance approval came through for Sabril. The medicine carried with it a risk of causing blindness. Being in sunlight increased this risk. We bought Skye a pair of baby sunglasses and had some success in keeping them on her. Per the manufacturer's recommendation, we kept the blinds closed at home to decrease sunlight. We lived in a cave.

Since Skye had now been seizing for a few months, I noticed the cumulative effects of the spasms. She smiled less. She interacted less. She didn't look at moving objects anymore. She started turning into a vegetable. The Cedars-Sinai doctors had been correct when they sat us down that day in the hospital.

I yearned to prove them wrong. There had to be a way to make this better. There had to be a way to fix her damaged brain. I couldn't breathe when I thought of spending the rest of my life in seizure limbo, existing rather than living.

The clusters of spasms increased in number. Some days it seemed that the Sabril worked and she had fewer seizures. Then she would have more the next day. I felt tired and lived in a dissociative state. Unable to process anything, I willed myself to get up every day and watch my daughter seize.

I had a mad desire to end my own life. I looked longingly at bridges and tall buildings. I thought of how many random pills I had around the house and wondered if the smorgasbord would be enough. I contemplated how easy it would be to plug up the exhaust pipe in our van and let it all go. I wouldn't wish such a terrible existence on anyone.

Skye's spasms occurred in the same way, in the same order, every time. Her eyes rolled back in her head and she flung her arms up in the air. The most telling sign were the tears that always left a residue beneath her eye. I watched Skye constantly for any signs of impending seizures or tear residue. It bordered on obsession.

During the period of Skye's intense seizing, my now two-year-old son tantrumed and stomped and yelled and cried and played furiously and manically with his Thomas the Train set. He demonstrated a loving and flexible demeanor, as well as a level of independence above his chronological years. His independence was both a luxury and a source of sadness. I needed him to entertain himself, but it felt unjust. He sacrificed so much for his sister!

I lived a rollercoaster existence. My days centered on watching Skye and charting her seizure activity. I felt on edge constantly. If I even suspected she was about to spasm, I tensed up and stared at her. I mentally prayed that it wouldn't happen and counted the seconds until the inevitable spasm began. When we had a good day, I smiled and read and called friends. When we had a bad day, I frowned and sulked and didn't want to talk to anyone.

Cortisol is a hormone that regulates our stress responses, amongst other functions. When a person lives with constant stress and hypervigilance, their body and mind suffer. Some doctors say that high stress is as dangerous as smoking or eating pork rinds for every meal. I knew my cortisol levels were probably way out of whack, but it didn't change the reality.

I met with a mental health therapist. She challenged a lot of my beliefs and behaviors and helped me process some of the trauma. I met with her weekly for about a year before we ended. One person can only do so much for another. She couldn't wave a magic wand and stop the spasms.

However, she provided a sounding board. I needed to tell someone my sickest, darkest thoughts. Adam couldn't handle them. One particularly challenging day, I said aloud that I wished Skye had died at birth and Adam looked at me with contempt. He chastised me like a child and it pissed me off.

I don't really wish Skye dead. I love both my children. I am lucky to have the privilege of raising them both. It's normal to fantasize about Adam and I waking up in a tropical resort, not packing lunches, running kids to soccer practice, and fighting over homework. I also wished I was taller, weighed ten pounds less, and had Beyonce's drive and talent. Is that so bad?

We increased Skye's Sabril dosage every week. Dr. Balke didn't like changing medications without a solid trial. Each person demonstrates different metabolic rates, drug tolerances, and severity of side effects. What works for one person might make another person ill. Dozens of anti-seizure medications exist for this reason.

Sabril is the first-line drug of choice for treating infantile spasms. It was worth increasing the dosage even though I worried about the medication causing her eyes irrevocable damage.

Over time, we increased the Sabril dosage so high that the pharmacist expressed concern.

"Is there a mistake in the prescription?" He pointed to her dosage. "This is the amount an adult male would take."

I shrugged. I felt we had no choice but to proceed.

After about six weeks on Sabril, Adam and I noticed the spasms decrease in frequency and intensity. I emailed Dr. Balke who expressed her delight. She told me to email her in a week with another update.

After another week, the spasms stopped completely! The sun appeared brighter and food tasted better. I felt glorious as I watched my daughter come back to life. She sat up straighter, smiled, looked around at objects again, and seemed less irritable overall. I relaxed an iota. I dreamed our life would go back to "normal."

I woke up each day looking at Skye for tear residue or twitching. I didn't see anything. I charted those days as "nothing." What a wonderful gift "nothing" can be! I told our friends and family and everyone cheered for us. I thought we had beaten epilepsy.

We had a wonderful, amazing month of being seizure-free. I forgot how it felt to just breathe. My brain had been locked in turbodrive for months. I laughed and smiled and played with Skye. I told her that I was proud of her brain. It had worked so hard against all the odds! We could relax and enjoy some time together as a "regular" family.

Chapter Twenty-Seven

And then, right when I let my guard down, it happened again. One morning, I held Skye in my arms, singing a tune. She turned pale. Her eyes rolled back in her head and she threw her arms in the air. A tsunami of grief rushed through my body. I said aloud, "No, no, no, no…"

I couldn't stop saying it as I gently placed her down on the carpet and looked up at the heavens. I felt utterly betrayed. I wanted to go up and rip out God's heart. A heart for a heart.

Experiencing that seizure-free month was almost worse than just experiencing the seizures. I tasted the dream and then it was gone. I saw glimpses of who my daughter was supposed to be, her sense of humor already apparent. And then the spasms wrenched her away from me. It felt cruel and unreal.

I grudgingly marked the spasm in her seizure log. Darkness swallowed me again as the days passed and the frequency of the spasms increased. I emailed Dr. Balke. She expressed empathy and sadness for us. Luckily, we got an appointment at UCLA for the following week. Dr. Balke told us to continue tracking the spasms and keep her in the loop.

The following week, we went to the UCLA Neurology Department and met with an epilepsy team. The doctors and nurse practitioners asked questions and suggested a thirty-six-hour EEG. With more data, the team could ascertain viable treatments. They expressed concern that Zonegran and Sabril didn't help.

We scheduled the thirty-six-hour EEG. While waiting, we continued charting her seizures. I put my faith in the UCLA doctors. I believed they would come up with some sort of solution. They spent every day helping children with epilepsy.

On the day of the EEG, we checked Skye in at admitting since she would be inpatient. For those unfamiliar with this process, picture this: When admitting gives you an arrival time, you will not begin your procedure or appointment at that time. You will sign your name on the check-in sheet. Then you wait. •

After a seemingly arbitrary time (anywhere from two minutes to one hour), the admitting employee calls your name. You follow their voice to a cubicle. They take a copy of your photo ID and insurance cards. You sign privacy practices notifications. You sign financial documents that state you are legally responsible for anything your insurance won't cover.

> **Fun Fact:** This can get ugly when you realize that hospitals charge $100 for a Q-tip.

Once you check in, you wait again. This wait can be all day. Hospitals never have enough available beds. A thirty-six-hour EEG isn't a life-threatening emergency so Skye didn't need a bed as desperately as the kid who just had a liver transplant. Similar to the airlines who overbook most flights, the hospital constantly shuffles and placates anxious, angry people.

We eventually got a room where Skye would stay for the EEG. The minimally furnished room held a small table and a bench seat that converted into a bed. We also had a private bathroom (my favorite feature). The room smelled like antiseptic cleaner and stale bread. Various doctors and nurses talked with us about the procedure and examined Skye. She sat in a large crib with a video camera hanging above it.

Skye screamed and cried while the technicians placed the electrodes and leads on her head. We comforted her as best we could. Stopping and starting made the situation worse for everyone, so the technicians powered through. I whispered in Skye's ear. I told her she was strong and amazing and that this would end soon. I told her we were all trying to help her. I forced my voice to remain calm and even.

Eventually the technicians finished and wrapped the top of Skye's head in gauze so she wouldn't rip off the leads. She looked like a Smurf. She immediately tried to remove the gauze. Nurses had to replace the wrappings three times during our stay. Skye never liked anything touching her head. I don't blame her.

The purpose of a video EEG is to show the patient's brainwaves and behavior simultaneously. Whenever Skye did anything abnormal or had a spasm, I pressed a button attached to the EEG monitor. It marked the time so the doctors could watch Skye's movements and compare it to her brainwaves. It helped confirm the presence of seizures.

During the EEG, we booked a local hotel for two nights. Adam and I each stayed one night in the hospital with Skye and one night in the hotel with Rowan. Skye didn't interact much at that point, so staying with her involved hours of one-sided conversation. I paced back and forth, while I constantly reread hospital signs and equipment warnings. Skye seemed just as bored. How many times can a person sing Old McDonald Had a Farm? The answer: a lot.

Nurses came in every few hours and checked Skye's vitals and general presentation. Doctors came in occasionally and asked questions or looked at the monitor. Custodians came in twice a day and replaced hand soap and mopped the floor.

Eventually we made it through the thirty-six hours. The doctors wanted to do a repeat EEG the following week. I couldn't believe we had to endure another inpatient stay. The team said they needed as much information as possible, so I nodded and agreed that we would return with Skye in a week.

I felt restless. I wanted a solution and I wanted it right away. I hadn't yet figured out the actual nature of treating epilepsy, which is essentially a cycle of trial and error and unknown variables. At the time, I didn't understand that epilepsy is a lifelong condition and we would never really be out of the woods.

Chapter Twenty-Eight

I lived in limbo, waiting for a magic solution to our problem. I joined a Yahoo listserv called Infantile Spasms and asked questions about treatment. I read the historical posts and noticed a theme. Many kids continued to have spasms even with treatment. Some took Sabril or other anti-seizure drugs. Some tried ACTH, a nasty steroid which results in death one percent of the time.

I read many positive stories about spasms ending after medication trials and surgeries. Supportive parents shared pictures of their grinning children who seemed to be making up some of their missed developmental growth. I also read sad and terrible stories about children who had tried ten medications and still seized years later.

Desperation jumped off the pages. When I read posts from years earlier, I yearned to know the outcome. Did anything help? Did the spasms ever stop? How badly was their kid doing now?

Every negative post led me to believe that our situation would end in an awful, gut-wrenching way. Thinking about Skye still seizing years from now made my brain collapse into itself. I barely functioned at that point. How could I live while my daughter continued to lose skills and personality?

Eventually, I learned to read posts and take a deep breath before jumping to conclusions. I educated myself and cross-checked information that seemed implausible. I reminded myself that people tend to write about their bad experiences online. When something goes right, we tend not to proselytize about it. We are too busy enjoying ourselves to bother.

A few people stood out as informal leaders of the group. Some of them had successfully stopped their child's spasms and returned to mentor us newbies. Some of them hadn't stopped the spasms and still managed to get up every morning and live fairly happy lives. Their message was clear - infantile spasms didn't define them. They had somehow reached the other side of acceptance.

I didn't know what to believe. The spasms stole my daughter's soul. I couldn't accept that my daughter might be like theirs with issues and problems and disabilities. I kept thinking of Skye as different from their children, as if she wasn't in the "severe" category.

Skye completed the repeat thirty-six-hour EEG. The UCLA doctors consulted and looked over the results from both EEGs and Dr. Balke's clinical reports. The team came into our hospital room.

"We found a focal point for the seizures, where they originate." The neurologist pointed to a spot on the left of his head. "We think it's right here."

Joy overtook me. Finding a focal point meant we had more treatment options. In particular, it opened up the possibility of surgery.

"Neurosurgery could operate and remove a triangular portion of her left hemisphere. They would take parts of her occipital and temporal lobes. In theory, by removing that part of the brain, the seizures should stop."

The nurse practitioner and other doctors nodded behind him.

"However," the neurologist said, "the neurosurgeon may determine she needs a full hemispherectomy. So be prepared for that possibility."

My heart dropped like an anvil. I had read about the surgery.

Several children on the infantile spasms listserv had undergone the procedure. A hemispherectomy meant total removal of Skye's left hemisphere. A person only has two hemispheres, so Skye would have half a brain! Half of her cortical material would be gone forever. I found it hard to fathom the ramifications of such an invasive surgery.

In the NICU, I had seen one baby seize constantly from birth. His loving parents and the boy's maternal grandmother sat vigil daily. A video camera hung over the baby's crib. Electrodes covered his tiny head and black sprouts of hair peeked out from beneath the white gauze.

One of Skye's nurses told me that the baby would probably end up having a hemispherectomy. When she explained what that meant, I looked at her like she was an alien from a faraway planet.

"It must turn them into lifeless blobs," I said.

"Most of them do quite well," she replied.

Now as the doctors mentioned the possibility to me, I thought about that boy and his family and wondered what befell them. What must his mother have felt? Did he ever stop seizing? Was he sitting in a corner, drooling and staring at the wall? Did he have any semblance of a life?

The epilepsy team felt fairly confident Skye only needed a temporal and occipital lobe removal and not a hemispherectomy. They didn't seem too concerned either way. We weren't the first people who received such news and we wouldn't be the last. We scheduled a consultation with the pediatric neurosurgeon, Dr. Gary Mathern, who would further explain our surgical options.

For the next two weeks, I looked at Skye's head and imagined it caved in and vacuous. She would become an absolute freak. I would never be able to work and I would never travel. I wouldn't be able to face everyone's stares and whispers. I wouldn't be able to avoid the gasps and frowns and pity emanating from everyone we came into contact with.

In the meantime, I read about Dr. Mathern's impressive credentials. They don't let just anyone cut open baby's brains for a living. Besides writing hundreds of esteemed articles about epilepsy, Dr. Mathern had pioneered a new hemispherectomy technique and won prestigious awards for his work on epilepsy. This guy was legit.

It certainly made me feel better to have him on our team. But so many doctors had let me down already. I had developed some trust issues. I tried to reason with myself. Whether I totally trusted this guy or not, I had to let him help me or we would be doomed.

Chapter Twenty-Nine

We met with Dr. Mathern in his office at the hospital. Impeccably dressed in an expensive-looking shirt and tie, Dr. Mathern sat across his desk from us. He seemed cold and detached as he explained the surgical options. He planned to go into the surgery assuming a temporal and occipital lobe removal, but he would perform a full hemispherectomy if needed.

Once he opened Skye's skull, he would place EEG leads directly on her brain. After he saw the condition of her brain and looked at the EEG results, he would come out of surgery and consult with us for a final decision. He would recommend occipital and temporal lobe removal or a hemispherectomy. We had to agree at that moment before he proceeded.

We signed a consent for all surgical options to cover every possibility. Even if he came out of surgery and recommended a hemispherectomy, we could still tell him no. As we listened to him list all the possible risks, I felt like saying no before he even started.

The odds of a successful surgery were eighty percent. Success in this case was defined as being seizure-free. Success was *not* defined as having a full physical recovery, because that was impossible. Some functions would never return.

If Dr. Mathern performed a complete hemispherectomy, Skye

would initially be paralyzed on her entire right side and would need extensive physical therapy. She would lose function in her right arm and hand forever. It would be possible for her to lift her right arm, but fine motor skills in her right hand would never return.

Her right leg would be weaker and prone to contractures and fatigue. She would most likely walk, but with a limp. She would need leg braces and special shoes forever.

She would have a visual field cut on her right side. She would never see anything on the right side of her body without moving her head to compensate.

Many of our speech functions exist in the left hemisphere, so removing that hemisphere would affect some facets of speech. Speech remained possible, but she would likely have problems with processing and articulation.

"What if we are the twenty percent and we cripple our daughter for nothing?" I asked.

I could barely contain my composure while asking. I felt like the odds were good, but it meant that some kids suffered horrible consequences and still had horrible seizures.

He shrugged and said he could go back in and remove parts of the right hemisphere, the occipital lobe in particular. Possibly, she would never be seizure-free. He said that the odds were much better with a full hemispherectomy versus partial lobe removal. But he emphasized there would be no way to know until he was inside her skull.

I hated his coldness and detachment. I hated him casually mentioning brain surgery like it was a routine tonsil removal. I hated that he couldn't make guarantees. I hated that he seemed so pompous and didn't have to make these decisions for his own children. I felt convinced that his children were perfect, privileged brats who attended fancy schools and ate caviar and lobster for dinner.

Now in retrospect, I understand the necessity of him staying detached. With a flick of his scalpel, he would cause us pain or joy. It was both a business transaction and a science. He shouldn't have emotionally attached himself to us or our child. I didn't want him struggling with the humanity of Skye's situation while he operated on her. I wanted him thinking clearly and rationally so he could make good clinical decisions.

I left the appointment with great hope and absolute despair. The two feelings played a horrific game of tug-a-war in my brain. Before this appointment, I felt so lucky that Skye's physical limitations were mild. She sat up independently, used both hands and both legs, and had begun the crawling process. I thought we had escaped the pure evil of spastic, useless limbs that can afflict people with cerebral palsy.

I looked at photographs of children stuck in wheelchairs with bent and contorted limbs, constant tremors, feeding tubes, and catheters. I felt like I was staring down my daughter's future. How could I render her arm and leg useless? How could I remove half of her visual field when her vision was already terrible? How could I make these decisions on behalf of a twelve-month-old?

She would suffer greatly and would never be the same. She would have to work harder than anyone to make simple gains in development.

I didn't, and still don't understand, why it had to be her. Why not someone else's kid? Or why not me? I could make decisions based on what I am willing to do. Maybe Skye would have said no to the surgery. Maybe she would have said that the seizures were better than dealing with physical limitations. Maybe she didn't want to take the chance of being the unlucky twenty percent.

These would have been understandable positions. But I didn't have the luxury of discussing any of it with her. I had to decide and I had to do it soon. At some point, the seizures would probably jump from the left hemisphere and affect the right hemisphere. They would become generalized. Our window for surgery would close and we might never find a solution.

I poured out my story and fears on the infantile spasms listserv and got responses from all over the world. Most people recommended the surgery and doing the hemispherectomy if it was indicated. Everyone said things seemed terrible at first, but got better.

One woman gave me her phone number and I called. Her child had undergone surgery but she had forbidden the doctor from removing her son's motor cortex. The surgeon tried to convince this mother otherwise, but she stayed steadfast. After surgery, the child still had seizures. But the mom said her son walked and used all of his limbs.

The woman said her son probably wouldn't have seizures anymore if she agreed to take out the motor cortex. She seemed at peace about her decision, although she seemed wistful.

I tried to take it all in and think as rationally as possible. But, I faced an emotionally charged decision. It seemed like the world might end in a cloud of ash, as if I could induce a fiery hell that would consume us all. I questioned my ability to deal. We could take our chances like the woman on the phone, but her kid still had seizures. I went round and round in my head.

We made a follow-up appointment with Dr. Balke in order to discuss the UCLA recommendations. I thought she might find the idea of a hemispherectomy preposterous. I secretly wanted her to tell me not to do it so I could get off the hook.

Instead, she expressed happiness that we had a surgical option. We discussed all the options with her, including trying other medications and the ketogenic diet. At the end of the appointment, I asked Dr. Balke what she would do for her own child. She said, "Surgery, surgery, surgery." She remained unequivocal.

"Do you want your daughter to have a functioning right arm or do you want to have a conversation with her?" she asked. Both, I wanted to scream. I want both!

"A conversation, of course. I want her to talk."

"Then you do the surgery," she said. "It gives her a chance."

She explained the rationale. Skye's brain damage was so extensive that it was unlikely we would ever control the infantile spasms with any type of medication cocktail or extreme diet. Destroyed pathways and scar tissue pervaded her left hemisphere. Essentially useless, the left hemisphere would always be at high risk for other types of seizures. If the brain tissue was gone, it couldn't cause further problems.

I told her that Adam and I would discuss it and I would do more research. She cautioned me not to take more than a few days. The seizures could jump over to the right side and then surgery would be out.

Chapter Thirty

During the next few days, Adam and I chewed our fingers to the bone. I barely ate or slept. The decision ultimately rested with us, but I wanted someone else to take my place for the next few months. I didn't know if I could deal with Skye's right side becoming paralyzed. Since she wouldn't understand what was happening, I feared for her emotional stability as well as my own.

I read gruesome details online about hemispherectomies. Skye's right eye would be black and swollen shut. Her entire head would be inflamed. The scalpel would cut over the entire top of her head and down the left side to her ear. She would look like Frankenstein's monster. Her beautiful brown hair with its lush, bouncy curls would be completely shaved off.

She would suffer pain and discomfort, but wouldn't be able to tell me. I imagined her writhing in pain in her hospital bed, looking like a plane crash victim with tubes and ventilators and bloody bandages everywhere. I would beg her to tell me how badly it hurt, what I could do for her, what body parts ached and itched and tingled. She would only stare at me with vacant, accusing eyes because I made her that way.

I read every online post and every article that even mentioned epileptic surgery. Adam and I talked about the pros and cons dozens of times. After a few days, we reached our decision.

We would proceed with surgery and would do the full hemispherectomy if indicated. Obviously we both hoped it wouldn't come to that. But we went with the evidence. Almost every scientific study supported the best outcomes with surgery versus medication or diet. All the listservs and case studies pointed to success with surgery. Even more importantly, all the mothers who posted online said they didn't regret doing the surgery. It was the only way to treat the cause and not put a bandaid on the symptoms.

We called the UCLA neurosurgery department to start the process. To my surprise, the scheduler called us back the next day and gave us a date less than two weeks away. It felt too soon, but once it was scheduled, it became real.

I called Dr. Balke's office and let her know our final decision. Her secretary scheduled us an appointment to further discuss the surgery and make a plan of action for Dr. Mathern. I called Skye's primary care physician and scheduled a pre-op evaluation and labs. We called Adam's family and told them our surgical date. His parents booked a flight from Ohio so they could watch Rowan during the first few days of surgery and recovery.

I touched Skye's right arm and hand often during the two weeks, savoring their softness and ability. When I looked at her, I felt immensely sad because she had no idea what horror approached. Ignorance truly is bliss.

Adam had a work conference in San Diego scheduled the weekend before surgery. We took the whole family and spent one last hurrah together. After the conference we would drive to UCLA, about two hours north of San Diego.

I remember being at the conference, talking with some of Adam's work colleagues and feeling completely disassociated from reality. Even though I formed coherent words, I lived in a dream world. No one had any idea what lay ahead for our family. I envied their ignorance. Many of his colleagues had their own burdens to bear, with their crumbling marriages, health issues, and dissatisfaction at work. I would have traded places with any of them that week.

The conference flew by more quickly than I had hoped for. We lingered as long as we could at the hotel. Finally, we drove up to L.A. and stayed the night at Adam's aunt's house. Adam's parents met us there and we settled Rowan in a bedroom with his favorite toys and books.

As usual, Rowan expressed no anxiety or sadness about us leaving for a few days. He delighted in spending time with his grandparents and great aunt. He was already an old pro staying in the city of angels. His acceptance didn't completely eradicate my mommy guilt, but I certainly breathed a little easier.

Between being in an unfamiliar bed and thinking about every possible horrible scenario, I didn't sleep well that night. Adam, Rowan, and Skye slept soundly. Getting sleep would have helped, but as usual, my racing mind was my own worst enemy.

Every sound startled me. Every creak jerked me upright. I sweated through the sheets. I felt my erratic heartbeat and felt my stomach rumbling. My whole body felt alternatively cold and hot and tense and limp. I couldn't get comfortable. Mercifully, I fell asleep at some point and rested my mind and body for the next day's battle.

Chapter Thirty-One

The moon still shone in the sky when the alarm rang. Everyone but Skye ate a few bites of food and changed into comfortable clothes. No use trying to impress anyone at the hospital. We kissed Rowan goodbye and loaded Skye in the car. During the forty-five minute drive, we listened to music and made small talk to distract ourselves. Neither of us wanted to dwell on the day. Skye slept on and off in her car seat.

We checked in at admitting and didn't have to wait long to sign paperwork and show insurance cards. Skye's surgery would take all day so she received a pre-surgical bed sooner rather than later. A nurse came in and examined Skye, took her temperature, and listened to her chest. All of her labs and physical presentation tested within normal limits. The anesthesiologist and Dr. Mathern came into the room to discuss the day's plan with us.

Dr. Mathern said that once he opened her skull and he could ascertain the actual damage, he would come out of surgery and give his recommendation. Once we gave final verbal consent, he would proceed with either the partial lobe removal or the hemispherectomy.

He cautioned us that it would be a very long surgery. I didn't feel comfortable about how long Skye might have to be under sedation, but the anesthesiologist assured us he would do everything in his power to keep her safe. I reminded myself that these guys worked for UCLA and had done this before.

Once they left, a nurse conducted one more check of Skye's vital signs. All the IVs would be inserted once she was under anesthesia. This news offered me some slight relief. Skye had always been a hard "stick" and she wouldn't suffer as nurses dug around her veins. She already looked like a seasoned junkie from previous pokes and sticks.

At that point, my stomach felt like a contortionist's playground. I couldn't catch my breath but I stayed steady and calm on the outside so I wouldn't increase Skye's stress. Still oblivious, she cooed and played with a shiny rattle while we waited. I watched the clock's second hand as it circled around, a subtle click marking each minute.

The surgical nurses came in and introduced themselves.

"It's time," one of them said.

They lay Skye down on the bed, covered her with warm blankets, and rolled her bed into the hallway. Adam and I walked with the team until we reached the dreaded double doors leading to the operating room. As always before one of her surgeries, I kissed Skye's cheek and whispered in her ear. I told her to be brave and strong and that I would be waiting for her when she woke up.

We checked into the surgical waiting area and received our patient number so we could follow her progress on the screen. The receptionist took down both of our cell numbers so we could be reached if we weren't in the waiting room.

Without much else to do, we found a spot with a couch, coffee table, *and* an outlet for re-charging our phones. Luck was on our side! I brought numerous magazines and books, crossword puzzles, a sweater, extra socks and underwear, and a small blanket. I wanted to lie down and sleep or get lost in a great book, but my mind raced and my body paced.

The minutes dragged by as I watched enviously as Adam read his book while relaxing on the couch. He slept on and off.

> **Fun Fact:** Adam can fall asleep standing on a street corner, sitting on a turbulent plane ride, or lying on a bed of broken glass.

I'm such a catastrophizer that during a turbulent plane ride, I grab the armrests and look around furtively while imagining my burnt, mangled body in the wreckage of the fuselage. So during Skye's surgery, I imagined her skull pried open with a humongous vise grip, blood spewed over every surface of the operating room.

In my mind, the doctors and nurses scurried around with blood and tissue splattered on their hands and faces. They screamed for assistance while running in circles, mouths agape. Bulging eyes betrayed their horror as Skye's blood poured down the table in rivulets and pooled at its base.

I couldn't get these terrible scenarios out of my head, so I played games on my phone and read every news feed I could in order to distract myself. The trashier the news, the less I had to think. For example, I remember being fascinated that, yet again, Kim Kardashian had "stepped out in a white two-piece."

The surgical waiting room filled up quickly and I found myself looking at the same people over and over again. This hospital, like many public places, was ideal for people-watching. Relatives waiting for their loved ones faced the same miserable situation, so an unspoken camaraderie developed. However, everyone also secretly judged each other.

Watching other families parent their children provided a great source of entertainment. Watching other people behave inappropriately in public also fascinated me.

One man planted his feet on a coffee table and fished out a pair of nail cutters. Is clipping your toenails on a shared coffee table a hygienic thing to do? One family put their toddler's smelly butt down on the floor. Is changing your baby in the aisle a smart move? A woman talked loudly and nonstop on her phone. Is sharing your personal problems with the world really how you want to spend your time?

Well, yes, apparently all these behaviors were fine and dandy.

I remember a woman wearing an inappropriate outfit, with six-inch stilettos and a dress three sizes too small. Someone smelled like cigarettes and alcohol. One family took up a whole row with their blankets and luggage, and sneered at anyone who walked by.

I sat by the door so I could also watch the hallway, which was swimming with interesting people and patients walking by. I saw an endless parade of doctors in scrubs, nursing students in crisp white, patients dragging IV poles and ventilators, scared moms, hospital administrators with clipboards and fancy shoes, custodians dragging garbage bags and brooms, kids using wheelchairs, crutches, and walkers, burn victims, cancer patients with bald heads and pale skin, teenagers with facial deformities and physical impairments, and kids wearing earphones, making weird noises, and screaming. Skye would fit in perfectly with this crowd.

Every so often, we looked at the screen and saw Skye's operating time. It read two hours, then four, then six. We stretched, walked, refilled water bottles, and twiddled our thumbs. Finally, the receptionist waved us over. She told us that Dr. Mathern was ready to speak with us. A hospital attendee led us up the elevator.

I watched the floor numbers and felt a lump in my throat. For once, I wished the elevator would suffer a malfunction and stay stuck between floors. Of course it worked, and when we stepped off the elevator, Dr. Mathern and two nurses stood in the hallway. Dr. Mathern looked pretty good for a guy six hours deep into brain surgery.

I could tell by his face what he was going to say.

"When I opened up her skull, I could see that her left hemisphere is already gone. We placed the EEG probes directly on her brain." He sighed. "It showed nonstop seizure activity on the entire left hemisphere. This clearly calls for a hemispherectomy."

Like a desperate criminal on death row, I tried to bargain.

"Surely you can save the motor cortex and take out everything else, right?"

"Skye's motor cortex is a mangled pile of scar tissue. There is nothing to save."

Dr. Mathern smiled. He looked into my eyes.

"Remember when we talked about all the possibilities? I told you that today would not be the time to make decisions. I can't proceed if you tell me to stop, but I don't want to do another craniotomy on your daughter in six months because she's still seizing."

He was absolutely right and I knew it. I had read the studies and talked to other parents and agonized with Dr. Balke. Dr. Mathern had seen the actual results over decades of doing this work and he was essentially telling me what to do.

Adam looked as scared and helpless as me. What else could we do? We stalled for a moment, but I thought of Skye lying under the surgical lights, her raw brain exposed. Every second we wasted out in the hallway meant another second she stayed under anesthesia, at risk for infections, complications, and death. I took a deep breath and told him to proceed with the hemispherectomy. Dr. Mathern nodded and he headed back into the operating room.

My tongue felt leaden. Someone or something else took over my body. I floated back to the waiting room and Adam and I slumped down in our chairs. I don't remember what we said to each other. Maybe we talked and maybe we didn't. I needed time to process our decision and its ramifications on our entire family. I still haven't fully processed it years later!

I knew that in a few hours our daughter would be paralyzed on her entire right side and would never make a full recovery. If she walked, it would be with a limp. Her right arm and hand would be, at best, a helper hand and, at worst, a useless appendage hanging down. Her language development would be altered and she might never utter a word. She might suffer emotional and behavioral issues as well as impulse control and executive functioning problems. She would never see a thing on her right side. And I chose to do all of these things to her!

Shakespeare himself couldn't describe the guilt and fear and agony. It was not of this world. As I sat in the waiting room chair, fatigue enshrouded my body and mind. A cocoon of denial and sorrow formed around me. I wanted to jump off a cliff.

Chapter Thirty-Two

When the operating time read ten hours, only a few people remained in the waiting room. Non-emergency surgeries usually don't start late in the day. Most patients are in recovery or already discharged by dinnertime. I grew restless. A nurse practitioner from our epilepsy team found us and sat down.

"You made the right decision," she said. "The kids with hemispherectomies have the best outcomes. They don't come down and see us anymore because their seizures are gone."

She smiled and it made me feel a tiny bit better. She assured us that Skye would soon be out of surgery and in recovery. We thanked her for the encouragement. Although it didn't diminish the chunk of terror churning in my stomach, it gave me some peace of mind.

I felt petrified that Skye wouldn't wake up from surgery. Like a cat, she had already beaten death on multiple occasions. I worried that her time might finally be up.

As the clock reached fourteen hours, I couldn't feel my body. The room smelled like old sandwiches and sweat. The words on my phone swam and blurred together. My mouth felt dry and stale. Food seemed unpalatable.

No seated position felt comfortable. Pacing and walking felt too difficult. Adam and I had nothing to say to each other. We were the only people left in the waiting room other than the phone attendant.

Finally, fifteen hours after we first settled in the waiting room, the attendant called us over. Dr. Mathern would be heading our way. Skye had been transferred to recovery. Yes!

I sat up and breathed normally for the first time that day. I knew that any number of complications could still arise, but I beamed with pride. Skye's brain failed her, but her body did not. She was tougher than an NFL linebacker.

Dr. Mathern walked through the waiting room door, dressed in scrubs. He looked haggard but he smiled. Walking straight toward me, he joyfully wrapped me in a bear hug. I was shocked that this cold, serious man hugged me like a family member. We later learned a term for this type of doctor: an "Oreo cookie." Hard and rough on the outside, he was actually a softy inside once he could show emotion. He released the hug and laughed.

"Congratulations! Everything went well and we didn't experience any complications."

Adam and I both teared up.

"So after these surgeries, the kid's brain essentially resets. I have some families that celebrate the surgical date each year as the child's new birthday." He nodded. "Makes sense actually."

We shook his hand and laughed and cried. Dr. Mathern explained that when she woke up in recovery, nurses would transfer her to the PICU (Pediatric Intensive Care Unit) for ten days or so. Then we would see if she had more seizures.

"I'm hopeful we got everything."

We thanked him profusely and he left, presumably to return home for some well-deserved rest. We waited until we were able to join Skye in recovery. I suddenly had a huge burst of energy and I couldn't sit still. I wrung my hands over and over. Fortunately, a hospital attendant soon led us up to the recovery ward.

After being under anesthesia, all patients move to the temporary recovery area. Nurses monitor vital signs closely as the patient wakes up. These patients are usually groggy, confused, and restless. No matter the type of surgery, being under anesthesia traumatizes the brain and body.

Once they wake up, the patient can drink small sips of water. If they handle the water without vomiting, the patient is allowed saltines or other light foods. Once they hold food down, nurses will remove IVs and leads. Patients then either discharge directly from there or transfer to a different ward, like the PICU or the regular floor.

Fun Fact: Skye always vomits after waking up from anesthesia.

As we came closer to Skye's recovery bed, I steeled myself. I had seen her head draped in full EEG gear. I had witnessed her newborn body entangled in leads, jaundice glasses, and IVs. I had watched her seize and called 911. But I remained terrified of what I might see that day. I felt afraid of my own child.

Nurses had bandaged Skye's entire head like a mummy. Her left eye was black and swollen, like she had been punched by the Incredible Hulk. Her whole body looked limp and loose so I couldn't tell what would happen when she awoke. I scanned the monitor and her vitals looked normal. She seemed at peace. I wanted it to last. I didn't want her paralyzed on her right side.

After a few hours, she did wake up. But, she didn't try to move her body much. I'm sure she remained in shock. Perhaps she couldn't even think about the right side of her body. Adam and I stroked her cheeks and hands. She hit all her vitals markers and transferred to the PICU. Adam and I helped her settle in bed and put her extra clothing and toys in the closet.

Adam and I did not have our own bathroom in the PICU room. Strangely, we had to leave the PICU ward and go out locked double doors in order to use the restroom. Upon returning to our room, we had to buzz back in and hope someone manned the intercom. Otherwise, we might be stuck in the hallway at two in the morning with groggy eyes, cursing our bladders for betraying us.

For the first few days, Skye didn't move much at all. The doctors had inserted an external drain into her head, which helped maintain the right amount of cerebrospinal fluid. Some children need shunts after having a hemispherectomy, but Skye already had one, so the drain just helped normalize her brain fluids.

The doctors had prescribed heavy pain medications. Two bags of saline solution hung from an IV pole. The solutions contained basic nutritional intake and dripped steadily into Skye's IV. I kept looking at her mummified head, curious but horrified about what it looked like beneath the white wrapping.

After a few days, Skye began to move her body and engage with others. The doctors stopped some of the heavy duty pain medications. She didn't seem distressed about her right side but I have no idea what she really thought. Physical therapists stopped by and examined her extremities. The doctors deemed Skye too young to enter the physical rehabilitation ward, so we would revisit that process at a later date. For now, they encouraged us to involve her right arm and hand in as many activities as possible.

At that time, her arm and hand hung down loosely at her side. The brain always follows the path of least resistance for its activities. Unless we manually moved Skye's right arm, her brain automatically used her left hand and arm. She used to suck her right thumb and use both hands almost equally, but now she only sucked her left thumb and reached for objects with her left hand. Like it or not, she was now left-handed.

Day by day, she grew stronger and more alert. Nurses removed the IVs and gave permission for me to breastfeed her. I crawled into her bed and contorted my body until she could feed. Imagine crawling into a crib half your height and twisting your body like a question mark. I dealt and made it work. Anything I could do to increase her chances of recovery seemed like a win for both Skye and our family.

After a week, the doctors came in to remove her head dressing and assess the sutures and healing process. I had stared at her for a week imagining her skull split in two, blood gushing out of her indented head. I had seen pictures of children with indented heads and it made me sick.

I didn't want people staring at my daughter like she was a monster. I didn't know how well I could accept such physical deformities. I wanted her intact. I knew her right arm and leg would be affected and she would never pass as "normal" again. I wanted her face and head to look normal so people would help her. I wanted to walk down the street without feeling shame. I feel horrible admitting it now, but it's what I thought about as the doctors prepared to unwrap her bandages.

Like Jack Nicholson's Joker in the old *Batman* movie, I held my breath and watched the doctor meticulously unwrap each layer of bandage. Instead of a physical mirror, I would be the judgmental object. I hoped for the best but prepared for disappointment. I have no idea what Adam felt at that moment. It is possible he wasn't worried at all, but I selfishly hoped he felt some fear too. Maybe I wasn't the only judgmental one in the room.

Finally, the doctor removed the wrapping. I looked at her head and… it wasn't as bad as I thought! Don't get me wrong, it still looked horrible! Skye's head did remind me of Frankenstein's monster with its massive, bulging sutures. Her shaved skull looked misshapen. Without hair to hide it, the shunt bulged out of her head. Her left eye remained swollen, black, and shut.

I detest a picture hanging on my in-law's bedroom wall. It shows Adam, me, and both children smiling for the camera. Taken shortly after Skye's surgery, the picture shows her fresh red and black sutures, raised shunt, swollen eye, and useless right arm. I look young and happy, but I actually felt aged and devastated. Throwing the picture in the trash wouldn't erase history. Adam's parents have plenty of other photos where Skye's head doesn't look weird and scary. But if someone saw that picture without context, I think they might run away in fear.

Chapter Thirty-Three

After a few days, doctors removed the external drain from Skye's head. Her shunt did its job and took over the drainage of her cerebralspinal fluid. Since the shunt functioned, her vital signs remained stable and her sutures weren't infected, the hospital discharged Skye after ten days.

We left the hospital unsure of what might happen. Although we hadn't seen a single infantile spasm, the doctors warned us that anesthesia can temporarily stop seizures for months. Once she reached three to six months post-operation without seizures, we would have a better idea about the success of the surgery.

Even with this caveat, I felt cautiously optimistic. Her spasms had been so severe and relentless before the surgery. Having even ten seizure-free days seemed like a miracle. Dr. Mathern was obviously pleased with this outcome and looked forward to seeing the long-term effect of the surgery.

We arrived home and looked around the house in wonder. We were entering a new dimension where infantile spasms might not exist. I shook the gray cobwebs out of my brain, and now I felt high on rainbows and sunshine! Even with this somewhat renewed lease on life, I found it impossible to completely relax. I tried, but I remained in a state of mild hypervigilance.

In technical terms, hypervigilance is a state in which a person feels on edge and worried at all times. Stress hormones fluctuate wildly. Some people have an exaggerated startle reflex, loss of sleep, and a sense of paranoia. Common sufferers include military veterans, victims of domestic violence, and witnesses to traumatic events. If hypervigilance affects work and relationships, it sometimes morphs into post-traumatic stress disorder.

Every time Skye looked like she might twitch, I held my breath in anticipation. I wanted to believe her spasms were gone, but I had been disappointed too often. If she seemed irritable at breakfast, I looked obsessively for teardrops throughout the rest of the day. If her arms looked like they moved at all, I stared intently at them for an hour. Living in such a hypervigilant state was horrible, but I couldn't shake it off completely. To this day, I still live in this reality to a degree.

Skye's shunt can malfunction at any second. She can experience another type of seizure. Her remaining right hemisphere also suffered brain damage. Tiny remnants of damaged brain on her left hemisphere might still be connected. She remains at extremely high risk for seizures for the rest of her life.

The medication protocol after a hemispherectomy depends on which hospital performed the surgery. Some hospitals allow patients to stop anti-epileptic medications the day of surgery. Other hospitals suggest the patient stay on medication for the rest of their lives. Every neurology department has different philosophies on treatment protocol. UCLA followed a conservative approach, so they advocated continuing medications.

Thankfully, the doctors stopped the evil Sabril and put Skye on Keppra, a generally well tolerated anti-epileptic drug. If the patient isn't one of the unlucky ones who get "Keppra Rage," it can work quite well. "Keppra Rage" is essentially what it sounds like: an irritable, angry reaction to a drug that is supposed to calm down the nervous system.

Once Skye returned home from UCLA, we gave her Tylenol and Advil as needed. She tended to lie down and suck her thumb for the majority of the day. After about five days, Adam and I agreed that Skye's crying and pain seemed to have increased in intensity. We took her to the local ER.

The ER doctors conducted a CT scan on her head. One doctor came in quite panicked after he read the results. He showed us on the computer that Skye had an enormous hematoma in her left hemisphere. A hematoma is a collection of blood, so it looked serious. The doctor said that the large mass probably caused her tremendous pain. He said it was a medical emergency and we needed to get her UCLA as soon as possible.

I experienced a terrible sense of déjà vu. The words "large mass" and "medical emergency" put me into a state of shock. I watched in detached reality as the doctor ran to a set of cabinets in the room and started grabbing random medical supplies

He predicted they would do another craniotomy to stop the bleeding, so he said he wanted to help prep her for surgery. He attempted to insert an IV lead into her neck but was unsuccessful. Adam and I stood fixated, observing the mad flurry. Everything seemed to slow down. I clutched a magazine in my hand. I smelled faint wafts of coffee. I heard light footsteps in the hallway.

Within a few minutes, nurses and EMTs loaded Skye into an ambulance which would drive down to the UCLA emergency room. They asked which one of us would ride with Skye, and I quickly said that I would. Adam nodded his head and said he would follow in his truck. I can't remember where Rowan was. If he was with us, he rode in the truck with Adam.

The ambulance ride was almost four hours long. I jumped in front next to the driver. An EMT sat next to Skye in the back where she was hooked up to a monitor, measuring her vital signs and blood pressure. One of the biggest mysteries of my life is how I made it through the entire trip without us stopping. I have never gone four hours without peeing before.

The driver and I talked about all sorts of mundane things like the weather and sports. It helped keep my mind settled as I tried to process the idea of Skye going into surgery less than a week after discharge. I thought she might die. I thought *I* might die. Shock, fatigue, or heart failure all seemed plausible.

The hematoma was so large, I didn't see how her brain could be salvaged. I felt like a fiery knife ravaged my guts. But I tried to maintain my composure for the seemingly endless days ahead. I knew from experience that I would need every iota of extra energy.

Chapter Thirty-Four

Once we arrived at UCLA, orderlies wheeled Skye into the ER and immediately took her to a bed. When a patient arrives via ambulance, the patient bumps the line and gets a bed right away. The EMTs called ahead and prepped the ER team about Skye's situation, so the doctors and nurses could prepare and obtain previous scans and reports.

CT scans aren't great for the body; they emit radiation and studies suggest that prolonged exposure to them can increase cancer risk. Skye has had more CT scans than I can count. It's not good, but such is life. She's an ER kid and I'm an ER mom.

Once the nurse hooked up her leads and monitor, she told us that the doctors would be with us as soon as possible. The nurse asked us the usual questions about current medications, medical history, and allergies. Even though we had stayed in the same hospital less than a week before, we repeated the same information that must exist in triplicate in their fancy computer system. This practice drives Adam crazy. I don't like it, but I am more patient.

Adam and I stroked Skye's back and looked at each other. Once again, we were the only two people in the world who could understand each other in that horrifying moment. We sat almost breathless waiting for Skye to bleed out, or for operating room nurses to come grab her, or for the blue emergency lights to start blaring.

Instead, an ER doctor calmly walked in and sat down next to Skye's bed. He spoke to us while he examined her extremities, touched her shunt to make sure it wasn't swollen, and looked at her vitals.

"So, those local doctors of yours don't understand hemispherectomies. They just don't see that kind of thing up there. This hematoma is a normal process that occurs after a hemispherectomy." He smiled. "They should have just called and we could have reassured them."

I almost jumped up and hugged him, but the huge adrenaline spike and crash just made me feel really, really tired. We were stuck back in L.A. for no reason. We had spent hours in our local ER and in the ambulance. We had both nearly suffered coronaries ourselves. And, we had spent hours wondering if our daughter would either die or need another craniotomy. It wasn't the local ER doctor's fault, but I really wish he had just called UCLA for consultation before he started shoving IV leads in Skye's neck. Sigh.

The UCLA doctor asked us about our pain regimen for Skye and laughed when we explained our "as needed" treatment. He explained that the mechanism of pain control has to be preventive, not reactive. Pain medicine should be given at a steady rate throughout the process.

Once a person actually feels pain, it's already too late. It can take up to a half-hour for Tylenol or Advil to relieve pain. Our nervous systems go into hyperdrive when we experience pain and it becomes difficult to bring the system back to normal. If the brain never experiences the pain in the first place, it can remain in a more baseline, healthy state. The patient will recover faster and be happier overall throughout the process.

We were essentially sending Skye into a rollercoaster of regulatory states and probably subjecting her to lots of unnecessary pain. We learned a very valuable lesson on pain management that day.

Eventually the doctor discharged us so we drove back home in Adam's truck. We were exhausted but felt relieved at the outcome. We could have shouted in frustration about the local doctors or worried about the gas money, time expenditure, and wear and tear on Adam's truck. But we didn't. We were beyond that point.

Chapter Thirty-Five

Over the next six months, Skye cried a lot and lay on her side. She flinched when we touched her, or moved her, or dressed her, or fed her. I could not cradle her body and soothe her. She pushed me away. I thought we had made a mistake. The only thing keeping me sane was the fact that she had no more spasms. We made the six-month marker as seizure-free!

One day, Skye allowed me to touch her arm for a second. She allowed this longer each day. Over the next few months, she sat up and grasped toys. She cried less each day and dressing became less traumatic. She made small gains in physical and occupational therapy. Her demeanor relaxed.

Her world consisted of a small square of space in our living room. We placed her in a seated position on a blanket in the middle of the floor. She had access to a few toys placed on her left side so she could both reach and see them. Because of the hemispherectomy, Skye could not see anything on her right side unless she physically moved her head. At that point in time, she hadn't figured out the skill of scanning, so if something wasn't on the left side of her body, it didn't exist.

Her right arm and leg seemed almost useless. Not yet clenched into classic hemiplegic posture, Skye's right fingers and arm hung loosely at her side. Her right leg seemed to be a heavy burden. She probably had a visual range of less than one foot. Her sense of hearing helped her recognize our presence. I theorized that she recognized the unique pattern of our footfalls.

For the next year or so, Skye stayed primarily in that same position. She didn't scoot, crawl, or attempt to stand. She didn't speak or nod her head. She grunted and slapped her chest when she wanted something. We interpreted her wants and needs based on guesswork and trial and error. It was very much like having a perpetual baby. She didn't have much emotion but she seemed relatively happy.

Skye's receptive knowledge increased but she had no expressive language capabilities. She became increasingly frustrated and impatient when we couldn't understand her whims. Partly because of this frustration, and probably because of some sensory issues and the missing parts of her brain, Skye began biting, grabbing hair, scratching, and pinching.

There is no more primal injury than a bite. It's deeply personal and intimate. The pain sears into bone. Adam and I were soon covered in bite marks and scratches.

I felt trapped and isolated. I didn't know anyone else going through the same hell. I met other parents who had children with special needs, and they had their own horror stories and sorrows, but their kids were much nicer than mine.

Our neurologist Dr. Balke watched Skye during an appointment and told me I needed to get Applied Behavioral Analysis (ABA) services or else Skye would turn into a monster.

"It isn't about what she's doing as a toddler," Dr. Balke said, "but what she will do when she's twenty years old."

I thought about Skye as a full-grown woman, dragging small animals and children to the ground where she would viciously bite and scratch them. I shuddered.

"Behaviors strengthen with time and Skye is intelligent enough to learn and change. It's worth a shot."

In addition, Skye developed another negative behavior that almost sent me over the edge. She began randomly uttering a long, high-pitched scream, usually in public places. The scream seemed impossibly loud, and was annoying and startling. I would have traded a bite on my inner thigh (indescribable pain) for even ten seconds less of her screaming.

I reacted too much and too often. I dramatically begged her to stop when she screamed in the grocery store or during one of Rowan's soccer games. She soaked in the attention like an undernourished plant. So, my dramatic overreaction only reinforced her behavior.

I felt desperate. I asked the Regional Center about obtaining services to decrease her aggression and screaming behaviors. I had read about the basics of ABA. It is supposed to decrease negative behaviors by directly addressing the cause of the behavior. The child might be trying to get attention, avoid a task or sensory overload, or obtain items. It can also be a maddening combination of these causes.

Skye loves attention, whether it's negative or positive. The more dramatic the attention, the better. When she bit me and I cried out in pain and yelled at her, she "won" because she got my attention. If I had ignored her when she bit, and then redirected her to a neutral task, she would have lost the magic of a reaction. In theory, this would lead to a decrease in the behavior.

I liked the logical concreteness of this system. Friends of ours had experienced varying degrees of success with ABA programs. Like every other service, the outcome is unique case by case.

I had many moments of exhaustion, bitterness, fear, and anger. I also had many moments of laughter, joy, hope, and love. Skye wasn't seizing so we were hopeful. She has a tremendous smile and I wanted nothing more than to give her whatever she wanted. She didn't talk or move much. It seemed as if she had a broken switch in her brain. We simply couldn't find a way to fix it.

The act of physically moving her around took a toll on our bodies. Every day Adam and I dressed her, diapered her, and lifted her into the bathtub, into her carseat, and onto the kitchen chair. We moved her from the bedroom to the living room and then back to her bedroom again. She is small-boned and short so we got lucky in that regard. However, she kept growing and Adam and I weren't getting any younger.

Through the Regional Center, we received in-home sessions from local practitioners including an occupational therapist, speech therapist, and early intervention therapist. Skye's speech therapist came every other Friday. Together, we worked to help Skye develop meaningful communication. She wasn't uttering any sounds other than grunts or cries.

One day the speech therapist brought a basket full of colorful balls, like a mini ball pit. It looked pretty fun to me. The speech therapist picked up Skye and sat her in the basket. Skye didn't react. She just sat there and sucked her thumb. The speech therapist looked dumbfounded and said that every other kid loved being in the ball pit.

She didn't understand Skye's lack of enthusiasm. I felt embarrassed and tried to explain and make excuses. I told her Skye wasn't enthusiastic about anything. The speech therapist was a nice lady but I don't think she ever understood Skye.

Skye's in-home occupational therapist and early start interventionist seemed better equipped to work with Skye. Over the next two years, they found new ways to motivate her. While Skye laughed and listened, they sang silly songs, played patty cake, and read adventure stories about brave little girls battling dragons.

Since Skye made progress and seemed to enjoy working with most of her service providers, I felt comfortable returning to work. We found a caring nanny who would watch Skye a few days a week. Skye's nanny and service providers patiently and methodically helped Skye gain social-emotional skills. Adam and I felt a slight sense of normalcy return.

I went back part-time to finish my therapy hours so I could obtain my state license. I didn't really want to work, and I especially didn't want to do therapy, which is exhausting even on good days. But I desperately wanted to finish the program, which required three thousand post-graduate hours of therapeutic services. Even more importantly, I needed a break from taking care of Skye.

Professionally, I saw countless clients, co-led therapeutic groups, and completed hours of professional development, supervision, and consultation. The three thousand hours shrunk down every day and I saw this number in the same way I saw Skye's CSF serum blood count - a beacon of light. At times, I felt barely present in sessions. At other times, the work gave me relief. Even though I couldn't save myself, perhaps I could save someone else.

Chapter Thirty-Six

At age three, Skye transitioned from having in-home services to attending public preschool. Many of her services would now be accessed through the school. She obtained a new Regional Center case manager and we said goodbye to our in-home therapists.

This is also when she obtained her first Individual Education Plan (IEP). An IEP is a legal document stipulating that the local school district is legally required to provide services to a child because the child has some sort of academic barrier. Common barriers include learning disabilities, ADHD, epilepsy, or autism.

A student has to qualify for services in order to receive an IEP. At times, parents disagree with the school's recommendations or feel the school isn't providing necessary services.

Skye has multiple severe disabilities, so she qualifies for services. No one has ever argued with me about whether she needs assistance. It's always the details that need ironed out.

During the initial IEP meeting, the team recommends placement in the appropriate school-based program. Since we live in a small area, only a few options exist. We don't have special schools for children who are blind, have physical impairments, or have epilepsy. Those types of schools exist only in large cities.

Our school district places kids with serious special needs into categories, such as Less Intensive, More Intensive, or Medically Fragile. The names change every few years but the categories generally remain the same. The district classified Skye as More Intensive. She was medically stable but she required extensive assistance.

Skye's preschool offered reverse inclusion, a practice where half the students were typical and half the students had special needs. The typical children modeled appropriate behaviors and provided instant "friends" for their classmates with special needs.

A certified teacher and multiple paraeducators staffed the classroom. While the teacher planned the daily lessons, the paraeducators provided direct care and interacted with the students.

Skye needed assistance with every part of her day. She would ride in a buggy at school and during outside excursions. She could stand for a few seconds, with her right leg bent at the knee and her right foot rested on its toes. It wasn't sustainable for long periods and she couldn't lift her own weight, so everyone mainly swung her around and lifted her from spot to spot.

On the first day of preschool, I felt pride and fear. I worried about Skye's shunt failing or her having another seizure. I stressed about her grabbing and biting other children and how many other parents might sue us. When we pulled up to the drop-off point, Skye's teacher and some paraeducators met us. Skye's teacher was new but competent. The teacher and I spoke on the phone a few weeks prior to discuss Skye and some of her needs.

Even so, the teacher and paraeducators had never met Skye. I walked with them, trying to fill them in on the extremely complex child they were about to work with every day. I didn't know it at the time, but the school district had a rule that didn't allow parents inside special education classrooms due to confidentiality. So the teacher followed protocol and told me I couldn't walk with her any further. I would have to request an administrator to join me in the classroom in order to enter.

How could I not go into the classroom with my severe child on the first day of school? My face reddened.

"I am not a helicopter parent and I don't need to stay glued to Skye's side all day. I need to tell the paraeducators about her shunt and her seizure history." My hands clenched into fists. "She bites and scratches and doesn't talk."

Even though I told the teacher all that information three weeks ago on the phone, the paraeducators may or may not have known any of that. The school district didn't pay for them to come in early and train for the students they were about to serve. Sometimes paraeducators get placed with a student who has a seizure disorder and they don't know anything about seizures. Or a petite paraeducator is assigned to a large student who runs into walls. Whatever the case, the needed information and training is often lacking.

When we got close to the classroom, Skye's preschool teacher continued to walk and repeated her mantra that I needed an administrator to come in with me in order to enter. I asked her who I should talk to and she gave me the name of the program specialist. Skye's teacher looked at me warmly and said that Skye would be fine. I hugged Skye goodbye and watched them walk into her classroom.

While standing on the school's blacktop, I started to cry. I tried to hide it from all the other parents wandering around the school campus. Most of them were a little sad too because a child's first day of any school grade is bittersweet. But they weren't sad for the same reason and I felt lost and angry.

I drove home and wrote an email to the program specialist asking for permission to enter Skye's classroom as soon as possible. I worried all morning and checked my phone constantly. Skye had been left with babysitters before, but Adam and I had always trained them and visually showed them Skye's idiosyncrasies.

When I went to pick up Skye, the teacher and paraeducators walked the students out to the parking lot where the parents waited. There were only about ten students so the teacher spoke to each of us for a moment about our child's first day. Skye sat in the buggy and we waited for the teacher's report.

The teacher said Skye did fine but she bit one of the paraeducators on the arm. They had to file a report with the school district because it broke skin. I shook my head, feeling shame and disappointment. I asked if I could speak to the paraeducator to apologize and the teacher told me not to worry. She said that the paraeducator wasn't mad and it wouldn't be the last time a student bites in a preschool classroom.

I waited a week and never heard back from the program specialist, so the district allowed another administrator to come into the classroom with me. Once there, I spent time with the paraeducators and explained Skye's behaviors and medical history. They thanked me for my time and information. The paraeducator who had been bitten told me that she cared for Skye and knew that I wasn't a horrible mother. She understood that being hurt was a hazard of the job.

Over time, I came to genuinely respect Skye's teacher and develop a warm relationship with her. I understood that she couldn't break rules on the first day of her employment with the district and let me in the classroom. She was a great teacher and worked tirelessly for her students. Skye stayed in her classroom for two years.

By my estimation, Skye had the most severe needs of any student in the classroom. Only one other child had an orthopedic issue and it was mild compared to Skye's. Other children bit, scratched, and screamed like Skye, but I would still argue she was the worst of the bunch.

Only Skye's materials needed to be adapted for her low vision.

Only a few children had special chairs, and Skye's was the bulkiest. Her special chair reminded me of a medieval torture chair with its complex strapping system.

The students were always nice to Skye but she never fully joined the group. The teacher and paraeducators always included her in activities, but she didn't have language skills, she moved slowly, and she had little desire to play.

During drop-off and pickup time, I watched her typical peers run around with ease, making friends and getting invited to playdates. I knew that none of the children were perfect and even the typical children had behavioral issues at times. But it still felt like Skye was the kid always picked last in PE.

By this point, I had somewhat resigned myself to the fact that Skye had disabilities, but it was excruciating for me to come to terms with the severity. During the course of a typical day, I forgot how strange and unusual her behavior actually was, but I always remembered when I saw her around other children her age. I forgot that not all children pound their chest, rock back and forth, bite their own hands until they bleed, and emit strange moaning sounds.

There were so many what-ifs at that time. I wondered what she might be like if she hadn't suffered a stroke. What would her voice sound like? What natural skills would she possess? How would she style her hair? It was an exercise in torture. I only know my daughter as she is, not as she might have been.

After her first year of preschool, Skye made small gains. Since she still didn't speak or express much, the teachers and specialists debated her placement for her second year of preschool. Her teacher felt unsure if she would develop her full potential if she lagged so far behind her peers. The school raised concerns about medical issues, like shunt failure or seizures.

I understood the teacher's point, but I had recently seen

indications that Skye might be poised for a breakthrough. She always had a spark brewing within her that doctors, nurses, and babysitters experienced when they spent time with her. Even her intense emotional outbursts indicated passion. We pushed for her to remain in the same preschool classroom for the second year and promised to re-evaluate placement for kindergarten the following year. I knew her teacher felt unsure, but I believed that Skye would surprise us all.

Chapter Thirty-Seven

During the break between the first and second years of preschool, Skye completed a stint in the pediatric rehabilitation center at Children's Hospital L.A. Normally this would take place immediately after a hemispherectomy, but doctors had deemed Skye too young at the time of her surgery. A few years older now, Skye could actually participate in intense physical and occupational therapy. Children's Hospital L.A. had the best inpatient facilities for such a program so we opted to go there instead of UCLA where she had her surgery.

Skye was admitted as inpatient in the rehabilitation ward. One parent could spend the night in the room with her. Since the rehabilitation program lasted three weeks, we obtained a Ronald McDonald House room where the other parent and Rowan could stay.

We brought basic belongings and toys for both kids. At this point, we had learned not to pack much. We always ended up wearing the same few outfits. RMH has laundry facilities, and hospitals call for casual, comfortable attire. When a nurse cleans up a vomit-spewed bed and then comes in to check on your kid, she definitely doesn't notice whether you have eyeliner on.

Fun Fact: I never had eyeliner on.

We drove down to RMH, where we would spend the night before checking Skye into the hospital the next morning. We parked in the RMH lot and I felt tingling in my body, like something bad was about to happen.

While walking into the building, I stared intensely at the walls and the office furniture. I smelled the building's bones and felt disoriented by the familiarity. My brain closed itself for business and I almost fell. Everything looked exactly as it did three years ago when I lived there while Skye was in the NICU. I felt tears forming and I couldn't breathe. Waves of sadness and grief and fear and terror rushed through my body.

I grabbed onto Skye's stroller and busied myself with her while Adam checked us in. I sang her a song, badly, and tried to breathe slowly. I stared at Skye and focused on her instead of the smells and sights of RMH. After a few minutes, the intense feelings subsided. Only a subtle discomfort remained. I knew it was a flashback, a stress reaction, a re-experiencing of a horrible time in my life. I couldn't believe how quickly it came on and how helpless I felt.

I had an uneasy feeling during my entire stay at RMH but the intensity decreased the longer we stayed. Also, we didn't have a sick or dying child this time. We knew Skye would leave in three weeks and be stronger. It helped those scary feelings subside.

The rehabilitation ward in the hospital helps children recovering from spinal injuries, major surgeries, heart attacks, strokes, and car accidents. Specialists design a therapy program based on the child's needs. Most programs include speech therapy, physical therapy, and occupational therapy every day, multiple times a day. Since the child stays inpatient, nurses take vitals and record all input and output. The hospital weighs every diaper and records every drop of water and food ingested.

Skye's therapists worked diligently to motivate her into working and actively participating. She had good days and not so good days. It wasn't a rousing success although she certainly gained strength and skills. Her speech therapist offered great suggestions about ways to increase her vocalizations. Since both Adam and I were there, the time passed quickly and without drama. We met multiple other RMH parents who commiserated with us about the challenges of raising a child with multiple disabilities.

I didn't feel fully relieved when we checked out of RMH and returned home. I made it through the three weeks without any more horrifying episodes but I never felt completely relaxed. As we pulled into our driveway, I looked forward to being home with my family for the remainder of the summer. It seemed so mundane, something that other people do all the time, but sweeping, cooking, and washing dishes felt joyous.

Chapter Thirty-Eight

Skye's second year of preschool began in a similar manner to her first year. She was still the most severe student in her class and she had low motivation. But over that year, three major changes occurred.

First, she began scooting. Using her left hand, she dragged herself on her butt toward toys and people. She made slow, tedious progress at first, but it was the first time since surgery that she moved with purpose. Suddenly we had to babyproof the cabinets and light sockets just like we did when Rowan was younger. It was a fabulous problem to have!

As she began scooting, we placed brightly colored toys around the floor so she had to move her body toward them. She delighted in reaching an object and would smile and laugh. Family and friends commented on her increased alertness.

Second, Skye started receiving Applied Behavioral Analysis (ABA) intervention services three days per week at home. Skye loved the extra individual attention. Our therapy team (made up of a talented interventionist and a supervisor) made it a priority to help Skye communicate more effectively. They theorized that if she could communicate better, she would feel less frustrated and she would bite, scream, and pinch less.

When the team first worked with Skye, she was four and a half years old and had never uttered a single word. More than one speech therapist expressed doubt about her ever talking. I envisioned myself learning sign language and teaching it to Skye.

Her ABA team began by teaching her to repeat sounds. After a few months, Skye began actively repeating every sound we gave her. In fact, "doing sounds" became one of her preferred activities. The team said "ba ba" or "too too" and Skye smiled and repeated the sounds. It enabled her to engage with others, as well as gain mastery over something. Plus, it seemed like she just enjoyed hearing the sounds coming from her own mouth.

It was actually fun! She acted silly and laughed, making the mood lighter at home. Once she mastered sounds, she moved onto words. She enjoyed repeating whole words just as much as the sounds. She especially enjoyed repeating food words, like "waffle," bagel," and "cheese."

With lots of practice and time, Skye began spontaneously saying the words "yes" and "no." Not only could she say the words, she used them correctly the majority of the time. I cannot overstate the magnitude of this new development.

Reciprocal communication still loomed far in the future, but at least we could ask her a yes/no question and receive an answer.

"Do you want eggs?" "Do you want the ball?" "Do you want me to sing to you?"

Even though the adult had to produce the choices, Skye played an active role in her daily activities. Once she chose a food, book, song, or clothing option, she smiled and her eyes gleamed with pride.

She still threw toys and food, bit, scratched, and pinched, but her high-pitched screaming stopped. I hated the other behaviors. I hated hiding my bruises and cuts. I hated feeling like a victim. Sometimes it would ruin my whole day and sometimes I let it go.

I watched her like a hawk around other children and adults and felt on edge whenever someone stood too close to Skye. But since her dreaded screaming had stopped, I felt hope that her physical aggressions might decrease or stop as well.

In addition to scooting and speaking, Skye developed a new physical symptom as well. She started having bursts of pain every few days. At first, I thought she was having a seizure. Her face scrunched up and tears ran down her cheek. I felt certain that her infantile spasms had returned. I wallowed in misery and started charting the episodes. I couldn't bear to talk to anyone about it because it was so painful to process.

But after a week or so of observation, they didn't seem like spasms at all. She looked like she was in pain for a few minutes, and then acted as if nothing had happened. She didn't lose her personality or stop smiling. She didn't roll her eyes back or throw up her hands either. Instead, her face flushed and she scrunched up the right side of her face, like she had eaten a sour pickle. Sometimes she looked panicked or cried.

Since Skye didn't have more words than yes/no, she couldn't tell us where the pain occurred, what it felt like, or how intense it was. We just had to go on observation and charting. Our friends and the school staff agreed that it looked like pain based on Skye's facial expressions and behaviors. Her pain seemed to cycle every few weeks, with multiple episodes a day for two weeks and then two weeks of pain-free days.

Dr. Balke didn't have an answer, but she increased Skye's dosage of Keppra in case it was a different type of seizure. She told us to take videos and keep charting.

Once again I had to watch Skye suffer and go through the process of realizing that nothing helped. We gave her Tylenol and Ibuprofen regularly, but neither drug is safe for long-term use. And by the time either drug worked, the "incident" (what we began calling them) had usually passed anyway so it was almost impossible to say if it had helped or not. We felt better giving her something versus nothing but it was an exercise in torture.

I'm not blaming her doctors for not knowing with certainty what was happening to Skye. The most probable hypotheses at that point included trigeminal neuralgia, migraines, or hemifacial spasms.

Based on these hypotheses, doctors prescribed various medications. Some of the medication trials served to rule out certain disorders. I read articles, perused medical journals, looked at listservs, watched YouTube videos, and joined organizations devoted to these various diagnoses. I just wanted an answer.

Any of these diagnoses consisted of debilitating symptoms. Websites devoted to trigeminal neuralgia talked about its horrific, lifelong issues. Patients shared their misery and their daily struggles to function. Unlike Skye, many of these patients didn't have a dozen other diagnoses. I found it increasingly unfair that Skye now had another issue to contend with.

With so many wonderful (and a few not-so-wonderful) changes in Skye, we looked forward to kindergarten. I loved the idea of having both my children in school at the same time. Our child care costs would significantly decrease and Skye would have more opportunities to learn new skills.

We opted to put Skye in a special day class, where she would spend the whole school day with other kids who have special needs. The class would be located in whatever elementary school site made the most sense due to space and number of children.

I can't speak to what works for anyone else's child, but for us, it seemed obvious that Skye would do well with a small class size, multiple adults present, and a slower pace. I am all for challenging a child and raising the bar, and I do believe typical children should have much more exposure to children with special needs than they currently do. However, I didn't want my child to be a guinea pig. Life was already hard enough.

Chapter Thirty-Nine

Some days I didn't think Skye would ever walk. She hadn't made much progress with putting weight on her right leg. She had a mild contracture in her right knee and ankle, where the joints had become stuck in a bent position. These can develop in people who have cerebral palsy, spinal injuries, or strokes. Skye needed to strengthen her legs and arm in order to stop more contractures from developing.

Since she needed as much physical therapy as possible, we looked into intensive summer programs. During the summer between preschool and kindergarten, we enrolled Skye in a private intensive rehabilitation program called NAPA Center. Located in L.A., the program used an intensive model similar to the rehabilitation unit at Children's Hospital L.A. NAPA Center would provide occupational, physical, and speech therapy five days per week for a three-week stay.

Our insurance company agreed to cover the cost because NAPA Center's treatment protocol could increase Skye's strength and functional abilities. Covering the cost of her rehabilitation could save our insurance company from paying for a lifetime of wheelchairs and physical therapy.

We did have to cover our own housing in L.A. Since our childcare expenses were about to decrease, and because Ronald McDonald House is an hour away from NAPA Center, we chose to stay in a long-term hotel. Since Skye wasn't inpatient in a hospital, our whole family relaxed. The hotel had a pool, hot tub, and a fabulous breakfast buffet. We stayed in El Segundo, a coastal town with light traffic and a charming downtown. Instead of feeling like a chore, it felt like a vacation.

During her days at NAPA, Skye cried and fussed while physical and occupational therapists worked with her. The therapists demanded a lot from Skye, but she engaged when they pushed her and learned her idiosyncrasies.

During speech therapy, she was quite interested in repeating words and playing with toys. It was definitely her favorite part of the day. Since she had no physical requirements, there was less stress for her. Seeing her calm and sweet during these moments was the best part of my day too.

She kept reminding me of how beautiful she really is, inside and out. She has to work harder than any other child does. Even though she protests and fights passionately at times, she is my daughter and I love her ferociously. It's why I haven't given her to protective custody after she bites me. It's why I wake up every morning and change her diaper and dress her. It's why I make her the same five foods in an endless rotation.

> **Fun Fact:** Skye only eats pizza, meatballs, bananas, bagels, and pancakes.

Overall, she made progress at NAPA Center in all areas. It proved worth the time and money. Our family certainly enjoyed our L.A. summer, with its perfect temperatures, incredible restaurants, and vibrant nightlife.

Only one negative marred the experience for me. During my downtime, I had to study for my final state therapy licensure exam. After five years, I had finally completed the required three thousand therapeutic hours. A few months earlier, I had passed the first exam.

All that remained was a second exam, which felt like the most pointless thing in the world. The exam required a special manual to learn how to pass the test. In no way would the test determine whether a person was a competent therapist. I found it insulting that we had to take it at all. And I had to waste valuable pool time buried in the stupid manual.

In terms of becoming a therapist, I already felt burned out. Skye's issues and the daily drain of taking care of her left me at almost zero in my emotional reserve tank.

I took the second test two weeks after we returned home from LA. After four hours of drudgery on a computer in a small room, the timer beeped. When I pushed submit and waited for the computer to calculate whether I passed or not, I literally grabbed the edge of my seat. I had studied and I generally do well on tests, but this particular test had a high failure rate.

The screen turned blank and I panicked for a few seconds. Then a fuzzy bit of writing. A green box. PASSED. I put my head in my hands and started to cry. I got up, signed myself out, and walked toward my car. Once I got outside, my crying turned into sobs. I knelt down because my body wouldn't function anymore.

I had spent the last eight years in professional limbo, working in a hyper-stressful field with crazy people. And that didn't count the clients. I left my children at home with strangers and compartmentalized my emotions about Skye while helping others with their problems. I heard horrible stories and answered crisis calls and made child abuse reports. But through it all, I had been in crisis myself.

As I sat crumpled outside the testing office, I knew that I didn't have to keep selling my soul anymore. With my license, I owned my time. I would receive actual monetary compensation for my work instead of "good experience" and "therapeutic hours." I had paid a steep price.

Now I just had to survive kindergarten.

Chapter Forty

I did survive the first day of kindergarten. But once again, I cried on the first day of my daughter's school year.

It started off perfectly fine. I dropped my son off for his first day of second grade. Skye sat in her stroller, perky and happy. We found Rowan's classroom, where he hung his backpack on a wall hook, and then ran to find his friends. "I'm fine mom," he told me, and I knew it was true. I said hello to a few moms and teachers, and then I sighed and walked back to the car.

I felt sad when I looked over at the kindergarten classrooms. I knew my friends and other excited parents and families waited eagerly with their new kindergarteners. They watched their children line up. The teachers graciously welcomed them with a song.

I knew that all the parents would take pictures of their capable children. Together, they would enter the classroom where their child would spend the next nine months. I craved that experience like a junkie craves heroin. I ached to walk with Skye over to those classrooms and form new relationships. I would have two children at the same school. I'd know only one principal and one set of secretaries. I'd follow one bell schedule, with one drop-off and one pickup.

But my fate held something different. I stood up straight and pushed Skye's stroller back to my van so I could drive her across town for her first day of school. I didn't look back because I might have started crying. It was a special day for Skye and I didn't want it ruined. Those emotions belonged to me and I knew it – Skye didn't care what school she attended, and she definitely didn't care about my ability to form new relationships.

We arrived at her school and the madness escalated. I drove past the already full handicapped spots. Damn! Every spot in the parking lot was taken, so I pulled out of the lot and drove down the street. Skye had just obtained a walker to use at home and school. She had limited endurance, but she could use it to maneuver and cover short distances.

I parked six blocks away. It might have been six miles since I had to drag a walker and push a piece of junk stroller that jerked to the right, which required a Herculean grip to keep it from ending up off the sidewalk. I already felt frustrated, but I had to get Skye to school. I opened her stroller, grabbed the walker, and tried to fold it up.

Since we just received the walker the week before, I stupidly hadn't learned how to collapse it yet, so I sat there yanking on it, trying to make it easier to carry. My growing frustration became palpable and, right on cue, Skye sensed my crappy mood and started growling and whining. I picked up the walker, slung the huge metal contraption over my left shoulder, and used my right hand to push the stroller. The alignment had magically worsened overnight and now the front wheel started to shake.

I made it one block and heard the bell ring, which set me off. I felt the tears well up. The walker hung on me, a literal albatross around my neck. As I approached the school, I saw parents and teachers loitering around the classrooms. All the parents wore annoying grins because their child just started first grade or sixth grade or whatever. I just had the same grin when I watched my son settle into his school.

I hated every single one of them and all of their perfect lives with their stupid, typical children. It only reminded me how isolated I was in the school, my town, and the world at large. Every single family looked different than mine.

These people didn't understand the true meaning of suffering. Even if their husband cheated, their job bored them, or their landlord hadn't fixed their fridge, they still didn't have to watch their child struggle every single day.

Their eyes turned and watched the end of my laborious journey. I was sweating by this point, exhausted from dragging the walker and stroller. I saw pity and disgust and curiosity, but not one smile or welcoming gesture. They watched the train wreck, but didn't have to do anything about it. They turned away once they got their fill, and I kept trudging along.

We finally made it to the drop-off area. Some genius administrator had placed the special education classes at the opposite end of the campus. Three children used walkers in Skye's class. All were screwed. None of them could make the walk across the long blacktop without tiring out and losing energy needed for the school day.

Skye and many other children in her class had after-school physical therapy, occupational therapy, speech therapy, and behavior therapy. Their day isn't like a typical kindergartner who goes home at noon, done for the day. Many children with special needs have hours of additional services after school. These kids need all their available energy.

The IEP team had previously discussed the issue of getting Skye across the blacktop in May. We all knew it would be a problem. I asked if we could drop Skye off in the back parking lot (adjacent to her classroom), but the IEP team squashed the idea. They said it would set a bad precedent. I can see their point. Pretty soon every parent will want to schedule a hemispherectomy so they can have preferred parking too!

We compromised and decided that the school would use a pushchair to transport her across the blacktop. A paraeducator would wait for Skye at the drop-off area with the pushchair. No one would have to use a baby stroller or carry her across the blacktop, risking a back injury. The paraeducator could push Skye to class and use the pushchair throughout the day as well.

But, on this first day, after all of our planning, the pushchair simply wasn't there. I walked up to two paraeducators who I knew worked in Skye's classroom. Like most paraeducators, they were enthusiastic and sweet. Paid criminally low wages, paraeducators face challenging experiences. In a given day, a paraeducator could have feces thrown at them, get bitten, listen to screaming, ranting lunatics, chase runners (kids who like to leave the classroom, quickly and without provocation), translate garbled speech, give CPR, or deal with seizures, shunt malfunctions, and complete meltdowns.

The paraeducators had no idea about the pushchair (not their fault), but one of them said she would go to the classroom and talk to the teacher. Skye and I were the only ones left who hadn't gone to class. But I waited because I wanted to set the precedent that was already discussed and planned for. Plus, our broken stroller was hardly up for the job.

The paraeducator returned a few minutes later with a very large, blue wheelchair – the kind that is used in the nurse's office for middle schoolers. The teacher had requested a small pushchair with a seatbelt, but the big blue one is what she had received.

I put Skye in the chair and knew immediately it wouldn't work. It had no seatbelt and looked comically big compared to Skye's tiny frame. The paraeducator put her arm around Skye and offered to hold her in that way so she wouldn't fall out. Her arm was an inch away from Skye's mouth.

"No," I said firmly, "move your arm or she will bite you."

I took Skye out of the wheelchair and put her back in our stroller.

"I will take her in the stroller today until we can sort this out," I said.

I apologized to the paraeducator for being short and frazzled. I tried to remain cheerful as we walked to the classroom, now about ten minutes late.

Skye's teacher was impossibly sweet and kind. All ten kids in her class had moderate to severe issues and disabilities. I apologized for being late, and took a deep breath. The paraeducator and I told her about the pushchair.

When the district dropped it off, the teacher knew it would be too large, so she said she had already put in a second request for the more appropriate pushchair. The teacher and I both knew that obtaining the pushchair would be pretty low on anyone's priority list.

We agreed that until we could work something out, I would use our stroller. The teacher said a paraeducator would meet us at the drop-off area. They would push the walker while I pushed the stroller to get Skye used to the routine.

When I picked Skye up that day, I walked to the classroom and put her in the stroller. The teacher said Skye had a good first day. She reiterated that a paraeducator would be waiting at drop-off the next morning. Skye's leg brace was in the wrong position so I adjusted it and pointed it out to the teacher.

No one in the classroom had any training about orthopedic impairments. If Skye's braces were in the wrong position, they could hurt her feet.

I took Skye to physical therapy that day after school. I clenched and unclenched my fists. My head hurt and my stomach churned. Skye's physical therapist, Linda, wasn't happy about the missing pushchair or the neglected foot brace.

"This is why they should have a physical therapist in the district," she said. "They would have made sure the correct pushchair was in place from day one. They could have trained the teacher and staff on how to fix her braces."

We agreed that Skye's teacher shouldn't have to chase down pushchairs and take a crash course on hypertonic muscles; she should be teaching my child and her nine other students. It seemed like an easy fix.

Luckily, our physical therapist had an appropriately sized pushchair in her storage shed. We labeled it and I loaded it into my van. I emailed the teacher. She expressed her gratitude and excitement. She knew as well as I did that the other pushchair might take months to procure.

The next day I took the pushchair with me. But, the paraeducator wasn't waiting for me. This shouldn't have been so hard! I just took Skye in the pushchair and threw the folded walker (I had figured it out when I wasn't frazzled) over my shoulder. I delivered Skye, the walker, the pushchair, and her backpack to the classroom. While I headed back to my car, I noticed the other two children with orthopedic impairments moving slowly across the blacktop in their walkers, both looking tired already.

At that point, I had dropped off the pushchair at school where it would stay. The paraeducators needed to bring it out to the drop-off area. Even more importantly, Skye would start riding the bus in a few days. The bus drivers couldn't legally walk Skye into her classroom. So if the pushchair didn't come out for drop-off, Skye would be stuck on the bus. I told the teacher and she completely agreed that the paraeducators had to be waiting for Skye with the pushchair from now on.

The next morning, the paraeducator didn't meet us with the pushchair. I wanted to spit fire at the teacher and the school. I imagined the look of fear on the teacher's face as I strangled her with the overhead projector cord.

I didn't have my stroller because I stupidly left it sitting on our front porch for use at home. Skye wasn't strong enough to make it across the blacktop in the walker. I couldn't leave her alone, sitting on the sidewalk by the road where she could scoot into traffic. She also picked up random items and shoved them into her mouth, so I couldn't risk her choking while I ran to the classroom. I didn't want to carry her the whole way because it would hurt my back and I would be scratched, bit, and pinched. The existing cuts and bruises on my arms already throbbed.

One of the other students who used a walker sat with her dad. We introduced ourselves. He waited because he left his daughter's walker in the classroom so he didn't have to drag it back and forth. A paraeducator was supposed to come with her walker, but no one showed.

We waited and heard the bell ring. Still no paraeducators. I called the school but nobody answered. The office staff probably had a line of students and parents to deal with. Skye became antsy and I worried she would have a meltdown and disturb other students who had already started class.

My friend Anna and her son walked by. Luckily for us, they are always late for everything. We asked her to tell the teacher that Skye needed her wheelchair and the other student needed her walker.

Anna's son was the third student who used a walker. We watched him make the journey across the blacktop while the dad and I entertained our fussy children. A few minutes later, we saw the paraeducators coming with both the pushchair and the walker. They loaded up Skye and the other student and we all walked to the classroom.

I talked with the teacher. I could barely keep my composure. I wanted to yell and scream. The teacher's face flushed and she ground her hands into each other. Her eyes shot back and forth, never landing on mine. She said the paraeducators would be outside the next day. I didn't trust her empty promises.

The experience represented the epitome of my special education experience so far. Overwhelmed and undertrained staff. Dumb decisions made by administrators. Rules put into place for seemingly arbitrary reasons. Education code cited as the excuse for every nonsensical decision. Common sense never seemingly used.

As I left the classroom, my friend Anna and I walked out together.

"Wow," she said, "this is really stinking hard. The teacher said my son has been fussy and low energy. It sounds like the long walk across the blacktop is too much for him." She shook her head. "I don't know what to do about it. How else can he get across?"

Both our kids had a history of seizures, as well as behavioral and sensory issues. Skye had a shunt. Both of us felt sad that our children didn't get to participate in kindergarten orientation like all the typical kindergarteners did. I don't know who decided it was okay to exclude our kids, but it only served to make us more defensive and angry.

Our kids should have been able to see their classrooms, the parents should have had the opportunity to meet their kid's teacher, and we all should have had that opportunity to meet one another and make introductions. Anna hadn't met the teacher until the first day of school.

I felt defensive and isolated. I had no idea how I would survive the next twelve years of dealing with the school system. I now understood my friend who audiotaped her IEPs, brought an advocate to meetings, and seemed tired whenever I saw her. I understood why a parent with a fifteen-year-old sent overly assertive emails, sued the district twice, and came across as angry and ungrateful. I felt overwhelmed and stressed and sad, and my kid was only in kindergarten.

I wished I could just sit with my friends, sip coffee and delight at how big and capable our kindergarten students had become. How jealous I felt imagining those other parents reveling in an ordinary day.

Chapter Forty-One

At the end of the first week of school, I received a phone call from one of our service providers. She had visited Skye's classroom to check on her progress and had been dumbfounded by what she witnessed. She had seen Skye's braces and shoes hanging off her feet, but the paraeducators made her walk anyway. Either they didn't notice or they didn't know how to fix them.

Walking with shoes hanging off is problematic for anyone, but walking with improperly placed braces can damage the feet and cause horrible learning patterns. I told Skye's teacher multiple times to check her braces a few times a day. I also sent her a video before school started, demonstrating how to check them. It was fairly simple to correct. It turned out the teacher never shared that information with the staff so they were unaware the braces were an issue.

Even worse, none of the children could reach their food from a seated position at the lunch table. The gap between the seat and the table was too large for most of the children to safely sit. Skye sat sideways on the bench and a paraeducator sat behind her. The paraeducator wrapped her knees around Skye to keep her from falling off. She fed Skye from her hand - not a plate or bowl, but her hand.

"It looks like a zoo and Skye is the wild animal."

The world seemed to close in on itself. I couldn't breathe. The classroom had literally become a circus and my daughter was the freak that everyone paid to see.

The situation seemed so obvious to me. The teacher had zero experience with orthopedic issues and now had three children in her class with such impairments. The district hadn't allowed us or Skye's physical therapist to help train the teacher or the paraeducators. We weren't provided an opportunity to meet the teacher or see the classroom during school orientation. We weren't allowed to enter the classroom on the first day. I asked the teacher five days in a row to have a paraeducator and pushchair at the drop-off and it didn't happen.

Fun Fact: This wasn't fun anymore.

If these issues had been better addressed before school began, I would have seen the ridiculously large table, showed the paraeducators how to check and fix Skye's braces, and discussed her shunt and seizure history. My child did not speak and had the cognitive ability of a one-year-old. She could not tell me when someone treated her badly or when she was in pain or how she ate out of someone's hand at lunch. These situations could all have been prevented.

I wrote an impassioned email about all of the problems and demanded they allow me in the classroom for training purposes. Before I sent it, Adam read the email and toned down the emotion, made it more concise, and added in some special education jargon. We sent the email to the teacher, the program specialist, the director of special education, the principal, and a few other people for good measure.

The teacher talked to me the next morning, her eyes wide and worried. She felt bad but couldn't explain herself. She had received her first hard lesson about working in special education. Parents throw grenades and the landscape is littered with landmines. But if they suit up in armor first, a special educator might just make it out alive. By not educating herself and preparing in advance, she set herself up for failure.

The teacher made mistakes and I wasn't okay with my daughter paying for them. My standards weren't even that high! I just wanted her teachers to keep her alive and safe. I could let almost anything else go. But Skye's teacher didn't inform staff about valuable safety information and she allowed my kid to eat out of someone else's hand.

The director of special education responded promptly and allowed Skye's physical therapist and I to go into the classroom. She apologized for our experiences and expressed her determination to help fix the issues. Overall, she demonstrated competence and was affable, warm, and engaging.

In all fairness, being the director of special education for a school district is one of the most difficult jobs. The director must work under the numerous guidelines of the Individuals with Disabilities Education Act (IDEA).

IDEA is a national law that guarantees a free appropriate public education to students with disabilities. IDEA has wonderful tenets, but, like any law, loopholes and phrasing put districts in a bind all the time. Most kids under the vast special education umbrella aren't like Skye. Many are high functioning and need simple accommodations like extra testing time, use of technology during class time, the ability to leave the classroom when needed, or special fidget toys.

After the emailing and meetings concluded, the pushchair and paraeducators began consistently meeting us at drop-off, so I put Skye on the bus. She loved the bus and the driver. My son rode the bus to his own school every day. I felt wonderful knowing both children would arrive safely at school, on time, without the stress of getting two children to two different schools that started at the exact same time.

A few days later, Skye's physical therapist and I went into the school and trained the paraeducators and teacher on Skye's braces, her walker, her shunt, seizure history, and her visual impairments. We explained how her issues affect where she should sit, how she interacts, and how to approach her.

I didn't need to spend hours with Rowan's teacher on the first day. Other than filling out the one-page "Get to Know You" form for the teacher, I usually just shook their hand and watched while Rowan ran toward his friends. Skye had a lot of intense issues. It's preposterous to expect teachers, bus drivers, and staff to somehow know how to walk with Skye, comfort her, keep her braces and shoes adjusted, and look for pain, seizures, and shunt malfunctions.

> **Fun Fact:** Every single school year, we get a new bus driver
> and new staff who know nothing about Skye.

The rest of the school year went fairly well. Skye threw anything and everything she picked up, including utensils, plates, balls, markers, paper, etc. The teacher effectively ignored this behavior and redirected Skye. We had a marked decrease in throwing behavior within a few months.

Skye's teacher and I got along and communicated well with each other. No other major issues occurred. Skye made progress and learned her colors and new vocabulary. I felt relieved that the situation hadn't boiled over. I really do hate conflict.

Chapter Forty-Two

Normally the kindergarten teacher would have had Skye in her classroom for the next three years, but this particular teacher got a job in a different district. We had a new teacher for Skye's first grade. She had decades of experience.

When I asked her if she knew what a shunt was, she looked at me and said, "Of course." When I asked her about orthopedic impairments, she asked how long we had been going to the medical therapy unit. When I asked if she knew anything about behavioral issues, she laughed and showed me scars on her arms.

Skye still had difficulty standing on her right leg during first grade. Her orthopedic issues straddled a gray area. She didn't need a wheelchair full-time, but she also couldn't walk without maximum assistance. If she needed a wheelchair full-time, I would have accepted that and gotten her the prettiest, coolest one I could find. We would have adapted our van and our house and made everything wheelchair accessible.

But the odds were in her favor. Most people with hemiplegic (one-sided) cerebral palsy walk independently. Most people with hemispherectomies walk independently. Sometimes the person walks with the classic cerebral palsy gait of shuffling and swinging the leg around, hand and arm tucked into the body. Sometimes a person uses crutches. But it's walking!

Skye went to physical therapy twice a week and Adam and I stretched and massaged her legs at home. We asked numerous doctors and physical therapists if they thought she would walk. Everyone said maybe. I believed that she would, but sometimes I wasn't sure. I looked into every possible intervention.

Skye's issues with walking stemmed from both spasticity and tone. Cerebral palsy and side effects from her hemispherectomy caused these horrible orthopedic issues.

Spastic muscles continuously contract. For a quick example of spasticity, flex one of your biceps. Now leave your bicep flexed until it starts feeling uncomfortable. Keep going. Imagine your bicep stuck in that position. If someone else manually stretches your arm, methodically and slowly, the muscles might relax and straighten. But as soon as that person lets go of your arm, the muscles return to the same uncomfortable, flexed position. Spasticity serves no purpose and can be painful and cause contractures.

Muscles with abnormal tone have either too much underlying strength or too little underlying strength. High tone makes a person stiff, like the tin man. Low tone makes a person weak and loose, like a rag doll. Both are bad.

Fun Fact: Skye has both low tone and high tone, in her typically non-typical way.

While I continued researching Skye's particular issues, I noticed more and more references to a surgery called selective dorsal rhizotomy. Selective dorsal rhizotomy (SDR) involves a surgeon opening up the spinal cord and cutting some of the nerves going to the patient's legs. SDR doesn't cure cerebral palsy. No treatment decreases tone. But the surgery can significantly decrease spasticity, which could allow her to walk.

Without surgery, the best way to reduce spasticity in the legs is exercise and movement. But if spasticity is severe, it's almost impossible to exercise enough to improve. Manually moving someone's legs doesn't strengthen them. Rather, it maintains range of motion, reduces the likelihood of blood clots and bedsores, and decreases the severity of contractures.

When I brought up SDR surgery a few years before, our orthopedic team scoffed at the idea and thought it too risky. But Skye had progressed and I produced better research, so everyone felt more positive. Even though SDR is an intense surgery involving the spinal column, the risks are relatively low and most children show improvement, sometimes significantly so.

SDR isn't a common surgery and not many pediatric surgeons have the experience to perform one. Luckily, a new, young pediatric neurosurgeon at Children's Hospital L.A. performed SDRs on kids with diplegic cerebral palsy (both legs affected by spasticity). She had never performed an SDR on a child like Skye with hemiplegic cerebral palsy (only one leg is affected). I am not a medical doctor, but it seemed to me that if a surgeon could operate successfully on both sides of the body, she should be able to operate on one side.

We got a referral to see the surgeon and scheduled an appointment. I waited with bated breath, terrified she would turn us down. I read her credentials and felt intimidated that we would be in the same room. I had to plead my case to a brilliant surgeon who cuts open kids' brains and spinal cords for a living. I had to convince her to cut open *my* daughter's spinal cord.

When we finally met in person, Dr. Kiehna was the nicest, warmest surgeon I have ever met. Relaxed but serious, impossibly smart and competent, she somehow covered all the bases while smiling and engaging me in conversation. I liked her immediately and knew this was who should perform my daughter's SDR.

We talked about risks and the fact that Dr. Kiehna had never done a hemiplegic cerebral palsy SDR before. She felt the same way I did; in theory, it shouldn't change the procedure or the results. But she consulted with Dr. Park, one of the gurus of SDR. He referenced several cases of hemiplegic children who had undergone SDR. They had achieved the same general outcomes as children with diplegic cerebral palsy. He felt it was worth pursuing.

Having a doctor, even one I really liked, open up Skye's spinal cord and mess around with its nerve roots sounded crazy. But I knew it would be worth the struggle. No surgery could compare to the stress and risk of a hemispherectomy. An SDR surgery could change not only Skye's life, but mine and Adam's as well. Carrying Skye around all day had already started taking a toll on our bodies.

The biggest challenge wouldn't be the surgery itself, but rather, the post-surgical rehabilitation. The assigned rehabilitation called for up to eight weeks of inpatient stay. This would occur in the same rehabilitation unit at Children's Hospital L.A. that we had stayed in earlier during her intensive summer program.

The website showed that the facilities had been newly renovated and moved to a new floor. But it appeared the unit had kept the same staff and daily schedule of physical therapy, occupational therapy, and speech therapy multiple times per day. I knew it would be physically grueling for Skye and emotionally grueling for me to motivate her.

When Skye completed the summer program, she had only stayed for three weeks. And I had Adam and Rowan with me. Taking Rowan to "normal" places like parks, museums, and restaurants gave reprieve from the daily grind of the hospital.

This surgery would occur during the school year, so it would just be Skye and me during the weekdays. Rowan and Adam planned to drive down for the weekends. Like the NICU experience years before, I would be Skye's primary advocate and caregiver. However, it would be worse than the NICU because during the week, I would sleep in

Skye's hospital room and be responsible for her caregiving.

I worried about missing Rowan, burning out on hospital food, and losing my mind due to lack of sleep. Skye never had problems falling asleep, but she always woke up in the middle of the night. She was never upset. Rather, she laughed, talked to herself, messed with her sheets and pillows, burped, and made silly noises.

Sometimes she stayed awake for hours. Sometimes she wouldn't go back to sleep at all. Adam and I took turns offering her water and tucking her back in. At home, she slept in a different room than us, so sometimes we could sleep through this.

Consequently, when we slept in the same room with Skye, nobody ever slept well. "Exotic" locations such as campgrounds, single-room hotels, and other people's houses became difficult for us to justify. We dealt when necessary, but Adam and I never functioned well the following day. Lack of sleep is a form of torture.

Even though I was signing up for two months of this very torture, the surgery could be life-changing. Eight weeks of hell in exchange for life-long improvement seemed like a good trade-off. If she needed to stay inpatient to maximize the surgery, then I needed to stay with her and deal with the repercussions.

Much of any surgical outcome is unique to the individual and their particular set of skills and motivation. Even though the surgery had been scheduled, most of the outcome would depend on Skye. Since the insurance company deemed the surgery medically necessary, it covered the cost. We had almost nothing to lose.

At that point in my professional life, I worked in private practice. I had the ability to move my clients around temporarily. I lumped everyone together, and then planned to miss a few weeks. I could keep my practice afloat by driving home every few weeks post-surgery to see clients. Adam planned for some time off work so he could stay with Skye on these days.

As a child, I imagined myself having a successful career. I obtained my master's degree in a calculated move to ensure success. But after Skye's birth and subsequent challenges, my idea of success completely changed. A work situation that allowed me the time and flexibility to be with family became more important than anything else. Never in my wildest dreams did I think I would enjoy staying home with my children.

Chapter Forty-Three

While Skye's surgery date loomed, I returned to obsessive, nervous behaviors. I couldn't stay off the computer. I spent hours looking at surgical websites, testimonials, pictures, before/after videos, and history of the procedure. I paced the house, cleaning, organizing, and detailing the cabinets. Because of my previous experiences in hospitals, I almost knew too much.

I knew the day of surgery would be long and tiring, scary and overwhelming, and numbing and dull. Having a preview of the experience felt worse than blindly entering the unknown. I reminded myself that after each surgery, Skye had experienced immediate, awesome results.

I replayed all the facts: I knew surgery was the right decision. However, she wouldn't have needed this spinal surgery if she hadn't had the hemispherectomy. I felt guilty about Skye playing catch-up with additional services and surgeries. I felt guilty for leaving my son again. I felt like the worst mother in the world.

I wished Rowan had a more traditional upbringing, where one member of the family didn't have such a serious disability. At the same time, I think it makes him a more compassionate, tolerant person. Since he has Skye for a sister, there isn't much more shocking or abnormal behavior he will ever encounter.

I spent as much time as I could with Rowan and tried to fill our days with enjoyable activities. For the first few days of surgery and recovery, Rowan would stay with friends so Adam and I could focus on Skye and he wouldn't miss school (not that he would have minded that part).

On the day before surgery, we dropped Rowan off with his friends. Then, once again, Adam, Skye, and I drove down to Ronald McDonald House. I didn't have the same visceral reaction that I had felt during my previous stay. Hey! I made emotional progress! We spent the night in our room while cursing the people next to us who seemingly threw an all-night party with noise makers, a full wet bar, and possibly cocaine.

The next morning, we checked in at admitting and obtained a pre-surgical room. After the nurses took Skye's vitals, Adam and I kissed her goodbye, and the surgical team wheeled her into the operating room.

We sat in the Children's Hospital L.A. (CHLA) waiting room, which is slightly smaller than the one at UCLA. We had plenty of natural entertainment. As before, we amused ourselves by observing other people's bad behavior.

Adam and I tracked Skye's progress while we read magazines and played on our phones. We took turns using the bathroom, grabbing food, making phone calls, and pacing the hallways. Surgery lasted over five hours, a bit longer than expected, but nothing concerning.

Fun Fact: Dr. Kiehna cut fifty percent of Skye's right leg motor neurons.

After waking up in the recovery ward, Skye moved to the Pediatric Intensive Care Unit (PICU). Her room was fairly large and, most importantly, we had our own bathroom! During the first few nights, Adam and I both slept in her PICU room. Sharing an extremely small couch, I slept with my feet in Adam's face and his in mine. Even with such sleeping discomfort, I wanted Adam to stay until Skye stabilized. I needed his assertiveness and strength for those first few nights.

During that first night, Skye vomited three times, violently and copiously. When she began choking and spewing, Adam and I jolted up, untangled ourselves, and ran to her bed. We placed her body on its side so she didn't choke on her own vomit. This was always an issue for Skye, so we didn't take any chances.

After she vomited, a nurse cleaned up the bed, changed the sheets, put Skye in new clothes, and tucked her back in. Adam and I laid down on our couch. I couldn't sleep a wink. Every time Skye moved or coughed, I sat up in panic. I kept picturing her throat filling with vomit until she silently asphyxiated.

In order for the incision to properly heal, Skye had to lie down on her back at all times for the first four days. Luckily, the PICU room had a swiveling television that could be placed above her head. She watched an endless marathon of *Wild Kratts*, *Curious George*, and *Frozen*. With the television and the pain medications, keeping her lying down proved easier than we thought.

After four days, Skye tested as stable enough to move to a regular room the next day, so Adam returned home. I wanted more time with him, but he had to head back north where Rowan and work waited. We said our goodbyes and I began mentally preparing for the long stay. Even though I had the couch all to myself that night, I felt more uncomfortable than ever.

The next day, orderlies ushered us to our new room. I put away all our toys, clothes, and toiletries. We would spend close to two months in that room so I needed to make it feel like home. I hung up pictures of my deceased mother, maternal grandmother, and both grandfathers. My maternal grandmother died a few months before Skye's surgery, so I still acutely felt her loss. My ancestors on the wall provided solace, strength, and inspiration.

One registered nurse and one care partner worked in each rehabilitation room. Care partners had a minimum of a high school diploma and CPR certification. They assisted with changing sheets, taking vitals, and monitoring fluid intake and bathroom output. Of course, some of these care partners were nice and some were jerks.

Unfortunately, the care partner we had on that first day fell into the latter category. Gruff, seemingly in a bad mood, and barking orders, she greeted me a few minutes after we arrived. I remembered her from our last time in the rehabilitation unit. Notorious amongst the parents, she was competent, but possessed an atrocious bedside manner.

Barely functioning from lack of sleep, I struggled to contain Skye's thrashing and pinching while we settled in our new space. When I saw this particular care partner enter the room, I almost burst into tears. I kept folding and putting clothes into drawers so she couldn't see my crumpled face.

Weakness wouldn't help me advocate for Skye in the long run. I needed this woman to see me as strong and capable. Otherwise, she would run all over me.

Chapter Forty-Four

After the first few days, Skye and I found our rhythm and developed a routine. Skye woke up early, and we played and watched television until the nurse entered the room to administer morning medications. The care partner took Skye's vitals and then the kitchen staff arrived with breakfast.

Skye then attended a combination of physical therapy, occupational therapy, and speech therapy in the morning. Unless a therapist wanted to show me a specific skill, they worked directly with Skye and kept parents out of the room. Sometimes all three therapies clustered together so I had two hours of time for myself.

During those breaks, I worked out and showered, grabbed coffee and breakfast, and walked around talking to other parents in the ward. Sometimes I could catch a short nap. However, someone entered the hospital room seemingly every few minutes, which kept me from fully falling asleep.

Someone might come and refill the soap containers. A nurse would stop in with a mundane question. ("Have you already ordered your dinner?") That evening's charge nurse would want to introduce herself. Maybe a ChildLife worker wanted to offer Skye a new toy. Every few hours someone would refill the gloves and bandages, or empty the trash. A doctor might even pop in, looking for Skye.

After a few weeks, while walking the hospital corridors on one of my breaks, I discovered a lovely meditation garden outside. Large water fountains blocked the view of the concrete buildings next door. I obsessively stared at the water rivulets cascading down the panes, becoming one with the pool below it. The constant flow of water seemed to represent life itself.

Four benches sat in the middle of the outdoor space. Flowers, bushes, and overhanging branches decorated the edges. I felt like a caterpillar, warm and safe in a protective sac. I smelled lavender and pine. A slight breeze kept the air cool and fresh, as if it had just stormed and everything rebirthed. I loved its energy.

The meditation garden looked nondescript from the hallway and its placement in an obscure area of the hospital meant I usually had the place all to myself. I spent many breaks sitting on a bench, breathing in fresh air. Sometimes I pushed Skye to the meditation garden and helped her touch plants and splash water. But because I needed the respite so badly, I usually just came by myself.

I spent the majority of my time in the hospital room caring for Skye or in the dining room, where the patients and families were encouraged to eat their meals. Although great in theory, eating together with the community never felt enjoyable to me.

Skye threw anything not nailed down. Silverware launched, food splatted, and plates flew like frisbees. Worse, Skye screamed and growled when I moved her from stroller to chair, while she waited for her food tray, and when she didn't like the offered food.

She rocked her chair back and forth, so I had to anchor it with my foot. And of course, Skye waited for the perfect opportunity to bite, pinch, or scratch. I had to monitor her vigilantly when someone passed by or sat too close.

She was a complete menace. I had to will myself to enter the room and maintain a moderately happy disposition. Other kids and families stared at us, and although no one said anything, I could see them avert their eyes when I looked up.

Some of the kids were more physically affected than Skye. One boy had genetic issues that meant he would never walk, but he charmed every nurse, parent, and child. One girl had a large facial deformity, but she sat quietly next to her mother speaking Spanish. One teenager's body looked ravaged from cancer, but she played games with her father and smiled at every person who entered the room. Every other child behaved so much better than mine.

I envied their lives. If Skye just sat in her wheelchair and drooled, I could take her anywhere. We could eat in restaurants, go to baseball games, travel on airplanes, and pick up Rowan from school without causing a scene.

Scratch marks wouldn't line my arms and I wouldn't feel scared every time I picked up my own daughter. Other family members could sit by her and not worry about becoming human punching bags. Our family life would look more like four members rather than three plus one at home with a babysitter.

I suppose that people would feel even sorrier for Skye and me. Seeing a child stuck in a wheelchair, unable to move their limbs, dripping spittle and snot, is certainly a horrific sight. People already stared at us all the time, but I think it would happen more often in that scenario.

In reality, I don't wish that life on her or myself. It's just a fantasy. Periodically, even to this day, I entertain the idea when I become emotionally exhausted. It would not be an easier life. It would be just like mine - heartbreaking and joyful. Skye possesses lots of skills and I love her extreme passion. I don't want her to be compliant and calm all the time. She wouldn't be her true self without some drama.

But back to the story at hand. After three weeks of being inpatient at CHLA, I started to go stir-crazy.

I felt like a prisoner. I spent my time looking out our window from the sixth floor, watching all the seemingly normal interactions on the streets below me. Shoppers walked into stores and bought food and trinkets. Drivers honked their horns and swerved around corners. Pedestrians used crosswalks and threw trash in the street.

Helpful Hint: When you start to envy the homeless and/or criminally insane, it's time for some kind of stress break.

From my window, I watched planes ascend and descend into LAX. Dreaming about the exotic destinations, I imagined a young couple traveling to Italy. They stared lovingly into each other's eyes while twirling strands of linguini around their forks, wine stains on their white tablecloth. Bits of tomatoes and olive oil lingered on their lips. They ordered more bread and wine because they could.

Meanwhile, from my sixth-floor window, the Staples Center loomed in the distance, surrounded by tall office buildings adorned with names of banks and Hollywood companies. I loved watching the blue Scientology building, known as Big Blue. It stood just within the field of view out my hospital window.

I developed a fascination with Scientology, partly because I lived temporarily near one of their famous buildings. Every time I glanced at the building, I marveled at all the people walking in with their white shirts and navy pants. How often did they audit? What did they do all day?

I have two college degrees in psychology. Scientology purports that therapy and psychiatry are evil. I like helping people and advocating for social justice, so I'm not really sure what Scientology has against me. I understand that therapy isn't a fix for all problems and that some people are perfectly capable of helping themselves. But I know that therapy has helped millions of people work through issues and problems.

A helicopter landing pad also sat right next to my hospital tower. I heard helicopters with their distinctive propellers when they landed and took off. I assumed that they were dealing with a medical emergency. I watched as they streaked across the sky and somehow always landed right in the middle of the red square etched on the rooftop.

Across the street sat a strip mall with a restaurant that specialized in both sushi and teriyaki, a smokeshop, a nail and hair salon, a vegan cafe, and a few random, nondescript shops. Vermont Street and Fountain Avenue provided me plenty of stimuli. I needed every bit of it so I didn't lose my mind from boredom and despair.

Chapter Forty-Five

Skye started spitting out her medications. Since she had rarely done this before, I felt annoyed and frustrated at this regression. She *needed* the medications for pain control, seizure management, and constipation reduction. This should go without saying, but it's dangerous to stop medications abruptly. Also, they must be taken every day at the same time.

The nurses did not help resolve this. Most of them exaggerated the situation by laughing, lecturing her, or overreacting. It became clear that Skye did this to exert some measure of control in her life.

She must have felt the suffocating rigidity of being micromanaged, poked, prodded, and tossed around at will. With extremely limited speech, she was essentially mute. Spitting out her medications was a very loud and clear way to say, "Screw you!"

I became so frustrated with the nurses and Skye that I told the hospital that I would administer the medications from that point on. Even though nurses would deliver the medication and watch me administer them, I controlled the reaction.

One particularly hard day, I sat in the hospital room with Skye. She spit out her medication for the third day in a row. I offered her water and she batted it away. Orange medication dripped on her shirt, pillowcases, and sheet. Skye laughed maniacally.

A nurse offered unsolicited instructions that only increased Skye's laughter.

"You should force her mouth open,' she said.

"She bites," I said.

Skye attempted to bite my arm. I had let my guard down when I paid attention to the nurse. I stormed up off the bed. I needed a break. I had nowhere to go, so I just left Skye on the bed and sat on the couch. The nurse seemed uncomfortable and said she would return later. I didn't blame her. I was falling apart.

Tears streamed down my face. I wanted to talk to Adam but he would have started his work day already. No one else could understand. It wasn't about the medications. It was about everything.

I couldn't call my friends with their typical kids. I resented and hated them at that moment. I couldn't take it if they said something like, "Well when Johnny acts out, I do A, B, and C." None of them have ever felt the way that I did at that moment.

I had no choice. I sucked up my feelings. I deposited them into a cavernous receptacle in my brain, the part that deals with trauma and pain and disillusionment.

I felt paranoid about being watched, questioned, and judged while giving medications and changing diapers. Every day a nurse or doctor told me that Skye didn't drink enough water. If anyone had ever suggested some magical way to force water into her mouth, I would have been the first in line to implement that.

During our stay, Skye endured "serial casting" on her legs. A physical therapist stretched her feet and ankles and put a cast on each leg. After a week, they removed the casts. The physical therapist increased the stretch, putting her feet and ankles at a slightly more ideal position, and then put a cast on each leg again. They repeated this for six weeks. Serial casting should theoretically increase range of motion, slowly and systematically. As with the ancient Chinese practice of foot binding, eventually the joints and bones adapt.

Serial casting increased Skye's range of motion, but she moaned in pain while trying to fall asleep. Grabbing her casts, she writhed around and tried stretching out her legs. The physical therapist said Skye probably felt discomfort because the casting put her ankles and feet into such a strained position. Without understanding why or how long the casts would be in place, Skye must have been confused and distressed.

I begged the night nurses to give her pain medication most nights. Especially on the nights when she experienced back spasms. A normal occurrence post-spinal surgery, back spasms are supposedly shocking and quite painful. For hours, Skye arched her back, rolled around in her sheets, and struggled to find a comfortable position. Sometimes she let me sing her a song, sometimes she pushed me away. Pain medication helped at times, but at other times seemed futile.

Heart pounding, sweat beading on my brow, I watched Skye struggle each night. Sitting upright in my couch-bed, I counted the days until this particular cast would come off and give her a few hours of peace. When she eventually fell asleep, I lay down and attempted to sleep myself. Even with my eyes closed, relaxing my body took a long time. I usually managed a few hours of sleep per night.

As our nights became less bearable, so did our days. I felt like I had a newborn baby again. I maintained a zombie existence on too little sleep. With bags hanging beneath my eyes, I shuffled my feet, barely brushed my hair, and completed a minimum of tasks. Skye suffered with low energy, irritability, and decreased motivation for therapy. Already a difficult patient, she screamed and fussed through most of her sessions.

Sleep deprivation and the psychological torture of Skye's suffering eradicated my soul. I felt like a shell of my former self.

A few days before discharge, I felt increasingly desperate. Digging deeper than ever, I found just enough emotional energy to carry me through. Unable to muster the strength to talk to anyone, I didn't check voicemails or social media. I needed every bit of reserve strength to lift my head up.

Reading a book or watching a television show seemed too taxing. I sat at the window for hours, willing my spirit to fly outside. Every person outside looked happy and free. None of them spent their mornings dressing a manic, aggressive child who should have been able to dress herself. None of them languished in hospital rooms, rehabilitation centers, or doctors' waiting rooms. I hated every one of them.

I survived the last few days. A doctor came into our room and signed the discharge order. Just as I had done years earlier in the NICU, I walked as fast as I could to our car. This time I wasn't smiling ear to ear. That would have been too much work.

Chapter Forty-Six

Over the next few years, Skye attended physical therapy constantly. She worked her way from barely sitting up, to using a walker, and then to using a crutch. Even though she needed assistance while walking, her leg stood straighter and her endurance was greater. She could stand on bare feet without collapsing to the ground.

The SDR surgery had been a success. Although it wasn't a magic wand that allowed Skye to walk with a normal gait, it gave her the opportunity to walk with less pain and for longer distances. She still needed assistance from an adult, especially when she transferred from her bed to the kitchen table, or from the shower to her room. Even with this assistance from an adult, the surgery allowed her more independence.

Skye had the same teacher during first, second, and third grade. Her loving teacher provided a structured environment with high expectations. Skye learned her letters, numbers, and shapes - something I never thought possible. Her language exploded. She could ask for help and told us when she was hungry, tired, or needed pain medication. Although severely delayed, her vocabulary grew every day.

Skye's aggressive behaviors decreased overall, but they stayed present. We came to the realization that ABA helped increase her communication but didn't do much for decreasing her physical aggression. No amount of behavior training could fix damaged frontal lobes.

We spoke to a psychiatrist who recommended different medications used for children with ADHD and behavioral issues. Since Skye began taking the medications, she seemed happier, calmer, and less aggressive. While her aggression and irritability continued to cause issues for her, we at least had a tool that helped.

Skye continued to suffer pain attacks of still unknown origin. The accepted hypothesis was trigeminal neuralgia, although that couldn't be determined with any certainty. We found an excellent doctor in the pain clinic at CHLA. Dr. Eugene Kim used a solution-focused approach and had an incredible bedside manner. He was intelligent, caring, and returned phone calls! We tried different medications and nerve blocks in her facial nerve.

The nerve blocks gave us merciful months where the pain went into remission. Even though the pain incidents always returned, Dr. Kim worked closely with us to find a permanent solution. Just having such a competent doctor working with us gave me solace. We were doing the best we could.

As of today, in fourth grade, Skye is medically stable and loves school. Her passion keeps me on my toes. She possesses a great sense of humor and we laugh constantly. She repeats words and answers simple questions. Listening to music and singing songs are her favorite activities. Although she prefers to play by herself, she asks for hugs, says "I love you" when Adam and I tuck her in at night, and holds our hands. When she isn't pinching me, she is the sweetest girl I know.

Adam's job provides great insurance coverage as well as access to some of the top doctors in the world. Because she lives with an educated, middle-class family, Skye receives stellar services, therapies, and medical equipment. Even with all of our privilege, ridiculous scenarios sometimes arise when obtaining those services, therapies, and equipment.

One example of such ridiculousness involves diapers. Prepare yourself for a tale of bureaucracy at its finest.

Because Skye has a disability and will be in diapers for significantly longer than a typical kid, the state sends her free diapers. Regional Center covered the cost of these diapers until Skye turned five. Then, Medi-Cal took over for Regional Center. In order to transition to Medi-Cal, I filled out an application form on behalf of Skye and sent it in.

A Medi-Cal representative called me and said that they required a letter from our insurance company stating that diapers aren't covered by them. I called my insurance company and requested the letter. A few weeks later, the insurance company sent me a letter saying that "urinary incontinence" is not a benefit covered under our insurance plan.

I scanned and emailed the letter from the insurance company to the Medi-Cal representative. She called me and said that the language on the form wasn't correct. It had to say "urinary incontinence supplies" were not covered.

I begrudgingly agreed that I would call our insurance company again and get the correct information written on the form. When I called the insurance company, the representative assured me that the new version of the letter would say "urinary incontinence supplies" are not covered.

After a few weeks, I still hadn't received the new letter in the mail. I called the insurance company and finally talked to someone on the phone. The representative looked in the system and saw a hold placed on the letter. She found no discernible reason why a hold had been placed at all. The representative released the hold so the letter could be sent.

Two weeks later I received the new letter in the mail. I opened it up and it said the exact same thing: "Urinary incontinence" was not a covered benefit. I called the Medi-Cal representative but I had to speak with her colleague instead. Her colleague looked at my file and told me that they never received any letter from me.

"Yes, you did get a letter from me, but your colleague didn't like the wording and asked me to get another one from my insurance company," I said.

She looked in the notes again.

"There is no letter here," she said. "That must be the problem."

"I will send you the letter again, but it is the exact same letter I sent two months ago and that got rejected."

"Send it anyway. I'm sure it says incontinence supplies," she said.

"It doesn't say incontinence supplies."

She sighed and told me to send it anyway. I sighed too.

I scanned and emailed the letter. The most recent Medi-Cal representative called and left a message. She said that the letter wouldn't work. Also, since they received two identical letters from me (hmm, so now they magically did receive my first letter?), Medi-Cal put in a request to my insurance company.

She said that the insurance company responds fifty percent of the time. If they didn't respond, Medi-Cal wouldn't fund the diapers. Sounding flustered, the message ended with the Medi-Cal representative saying that our insurance company always sends letters with the correct wording, so she couldn't understand why I wasn't receiving the correct letter.

Assuming that our insurance company wouldn't respond, I called and talked to my third insurance representative about the diaper issue. I explained my predicament while the representative looked over our case notes. She said that letters were computer-generated so she didn't think it could include the specific wording Medi-Cal required. But she put in the request anyway.

I called back Medi-Cal and talked to my original representative, explaining the newest development. She thanked me for being so "on it," and echoed the statement that she couldn't understand how other clients have gotten letters from my insurance company that have the correct language.

I repeated what the insurance representative told me. I asked why the Medi-Cal representative couldn't just check the eligibility box. She laughed. I wasn't joking. Everyone obviously knew that the diapers weren't covered by our insurance company.

A few weeks later, I received the third letter from our insurance company. It read "incontinence supplies" were not covered. Finally, we had a letter with the correct wording! After scanning and emailing the letter to Medi-Cal, an email response arrived stating Medi-Cal would take over funding for Skye's diapers.

So many systemic issues slowed down the process. Why couldn't our insurance company send letters via email instead of snail mail? Why did the original letter "disappear" and "reappear" from Medi-Cal's system? Why did the third letter have the correct wording, but not the first two? Why did the insurance company only bother to respond half the time when asked for assistance by Medi-Cal? Why did I have to deal with two different Medi-Cal representatives, muddling efficiency and increasing frustration?

Fun Fact: Dealing with government agencies and county departments is as enjoyable as licking pavement.

Chapter Forty-Seven

Some disabilities appear mild or hardly noticeable. Cognitive or behavior issues might lie hidden beneath a typically functioning body. These children and parents don't always receive help and sympathy from others. Sometimes the child isn't severe enough to qualify for services.

As of this writing, Skye is nine. I am one of the most judgmental people concerning children with mild disabilities. I've had this same conversation many times:

"Oh, your daughter is lovely. I understand completely. My son has special needs too."

"Oh what's his disability?" I ask.

"He's got a learning disability. Sometimes he loses focus in class, so I might have to take him out of the honors level."

If I hear the words "high functioning" one more time, I might vomit. We aren't even living on the same planet. Forget about Honors English; my kid can't even hold a pen.

Sometimes I feel like the loneliest mom on the planet. When I watch my friends with their new babies and toddlers, I simultaneously feel happy for them and sad for myself and Skye. I struggle while watching their children meet milestones and gain an open invite to the regular world that my child will never enter.

It's difficult to care when I watch a new mother friend struggle with mundane issues that I know will pass: a newborn sleeping poorly, potty training setbacks, separation anxiety, the first day of preschool, diaper blowouts, backaches from carrying kids and strollers and extra bags.

I don't enjoy watching my friends suffer, but those first few years are so fleeting. Just as quickly as it comes on, the child sleeps and wipes their own butt and plays independently and carries their own backpack to school. Nine years later, I still change diapers and wipe butts, carry strollers and extra bags, and lament my inability to sleep in. I'm not a martyr, but I'm running a marathon, not a sprint.

I have a low tolerance for incompetence. I realize I'm not perfect, but I feel annoyed when other adults with seemingly easy lives can't complete easy tasks. When I walk into a friend's house and I see piles of laundry, mail, and dishes everywhere, I don't judge the mess. Sometimes my house looks like a bomb exploded inside. I *do* judge when the person arrives late, flakes out on plans, lets easy projects go unfinished - and blames it on their typical son's "packed" schedule.

All of us could benefit from looking at what constitutes an everyday "problem." I wonder about typical children who walk and talk and entertain themselves. What do their parents do all day? Do they sip wine on chaise lounges while their child essentially takes care of himself? Do they ride atop elephants and eat in fancy restaurants every night? Judging from social media, it sure seems like it.

I recently read a Hollywood star's memoir about her life. While pregnant, the star went into preterm labor. Doctors speculated that her baby might have abnormalities. She described her panic and concern about having a baby who wasn't *normal.*

Her reaction was perfectly reasonable. I didn't want a kid with special needs either, so I'm not going to pretend I jumped for joy when I found out. But, I resent the insinuation that comes with the word *normal.*

When people say they want a healthy baby, I understand what they mean. But sometimes I feel like it negates my daughter and our experience. No one has ever called my daughter normal. I've known since my problematic ultrasound that I would have an abnormal experience. But even an abnormal experience can be a worthwhile experience.

I know that Hollywood star may not believe this, but if her son hadn't been *normal*, she would have loved him just as fiercely. I naïvely wish that she had included something hopeful, like, "I was ready to accept anything," or, "I welcomed my beautiful baby boy no matter what."

Ironically, she's not a bad choice to parent a child with special needs. With resources, money, and influence, her child would have had more privilege than most. Obviously, she doesn't deserve to have a kid with special needs just because she's rich. But she would've been equipped to deal with it.

I'm happy for the star that her son turned out *normal*. She never mentioned the medical scare again. She didn't have to. I guess a person can't appreciate what they have without experiencing it another way. I shouldn't expect such introspection. Even my good friends don't get it.

One of my good friends and I were talking on the phone a few years ago. Sharing details about a trip she and her kids had taken, my friend explained how much fun they had together. I agreed that nothing beats having fun as a family.

"Well I'm sure you have fun times with Rowan," she said.

"Yes I do, but I also have fun times with Skye."

"Oh, I didn't know that. I thought maybe you didn't."

I felt incredulous that she assumed I didn't have fun with Skye. My god, does everyone think it's that bad?

We are first and foremost a family. Skye's disabilities affect us all

214

the time, each and every day. But we are more like other families than we are different. We eat dinner, pack lunches, drag kids to sports practices and music lessons, juggle birthday parties and work obligations, go swimming, and negotiate screen time.

My friend reminded me that Skye looked awful the last time she saw her, when Skye was eleven months old. At that time, Skye suffered daily seizures, essentially turning her into a zombie. Wow, Skye had changed so much since that time.

I know people feel sorry for me, but people also overestimate the agony and underestimate the joy. I assured my friend that I actually *do* have fun with Skye. It's not all horror and sadness. Gray cobwebs aren't draped over every surface. I don't lie around sobbing and writhing on the ground in desperation. Sometimes I do sob and life seems horrible. But, I told her, that's life. Sometimes it's full of rainbows and unicorns too.

Chapter Forty-Eight

Emily Perl Kingsley wrote a beautiful anecdote entitled *Welcome to Holland* about a journey of acceptance. Acceptance of one's child, acceptance of one's circumstances, and acceptance of one's new normal.

Welcome to Holland compares the anticipation of giving birth to the anticipation of an upcoming vacation to Italy. While dreaming of Italy and everything they will experience in that magical country, the narrator boards her flight with bags in hand.

Unexpectedly, the plane lands in Holland instead of Italy. Confused and disappointed because everyone else on the plane continued onto Italy, the narrator must learn about Holland with its different pace and language. Eventually, the narrator learns to appreciate the wonders of Holland and reaches bittersweet acceptance.

I have mixed feelings about this anecdote. Many school professionals, therapists, friends, and nurses pass it out when they encounter a parent who has a child with special needs. Some parents love this anecdote, and swear it helped them in time of great need. Other parents feel it under-represents the challenges of raising such a child.

I discuss the anecdote here because it causes such a dichotomous reaction in the special needs community. If a person searches

"Welcome to Holland," dozens of blog posts and essays appear touting both its magnificence and its problematic message.

When Skye stayed in the NICU, a friend recommended that I read "Welcome to Holland." She figured I would relate. I searched for it on my phone. By the fourth line, I shook my head. When I finished reading, I threw my phone to the side and huffed and puffed. I may have stamped my feet a little.

So I'm in Holland! Get real. Let's pretend you had packed your bags for Italy, with guidebooks in your pocket, and a memorized list of exquisite restaurants. You told EVERYONE about your trip and how AWESOME it would be. When your plane landed, you exited and saw a large banner. It read, "Welcome to Holland!" I bet you would huff and puff and stamp your feet too.

In time, I would visit the metaphorical Amsterdam, including Anne Frank's house, the Van Gogh museum, and every tulip garden. But when I first disembarked from the plane in Holland, I had to watch everyone else continue to Italy. None of them knew how excruciating it felt to be left behind while they sipped Italian wine and ate ravioli for dinner. I, however, ate breakfast, lunch, and dinner in the Holland NICU.

I don't really have anything against Holland. Obviously the "Welcome to Holland" anecdote is a metaphor for reaching acceptance and seeing the truly wonderful things inherent in our children. I agree with the author that focusing on disappointment is counterproductive. Our children are worthy of acceptance and love.

However, I wasn't ready to read it while we stayed in the NICU. I didn't want to accept the monstrosity of a child I created. I felt resentful that the author packaged so much hurt and anger and sadness into a cloying metaphor. All the emotions felt so much bigger than a one-page essay.

Although I respect the author, I viscerally react when I see the anecdote in print. I sometimes resent the parents who wine and dine in Italy. Since I associate it with such a dark time, it offers me little solace.

I never knew my daughter before her stroke, but it's easy to imagine what might have been. I imagine it every time I see a girl her age running around with cute leggings, stylish boots, and a serene smile. The girl looks up at her mother, curly locks hanging over her eyes. With two working arms, she picks up a ball and plays catch with her friends. With two working legs, she runs and twirls and does cartwheels. Her clear, crisp speaking voice echoes over the playground.

Thinking this way isn't fair to Skye. It's also irrational. Imagining what Skye would have been like doesn't change anything. It makes me feel depressed, angry, sad, and jealous. Sometimes I can't bear to watch a group of girls running and playing and laughing. I feel too sad. Sometimes I watch them play and I smile because Skye is their age.

I have a fabulous daughter. I believe this is where "Welcome to Holland" helps. Like Holland, Skye is worthy of admiration. While it is true that most other parents continued onto Italy, I still have the privilege of exploring Holland. Like Holland, Skye is worthy of admiration. She is not inferior, just different.

Skye is genuine and funny. She is uninterested in gossip or tearing other people down. Quite charming when she wants to be, Skye can make the world seem magical. Every morning I go into her room to help her get ready for the day. When I walk into the room, her smile widens and she bounces with joy. It's wonderful to feel such unconditional love.

I strive to accept having a daughter with multiple severe disabilities. There must be a reason I am Skye's mother. There must be a reason that Skye suffers. If not, then it turns the whole matrix on its head.

Chapter Forty-Nine

Some people say having their child with special needs has been nothing but joyful and wonderful. They can't imagine their child any different. They wouldn't change their child if they could. I have met other parents who say the situation is dire. They feel no joy. They say nothing good comes from it. If someone offered to change their child, they would jump at the chance.

I fit somewhere in the middle of these polarities. My life is full of joy. I love watching movies with my family, cooking elaborate meals, and walking with friends. I enjoy spending time with Skye. I sing songs with goofy lyrics, tickle her belly, and make funny faces. She rewards me with the most genuine laugh I've ever heard.

Skye lives in the present moment at all times. She never regrets the past or worries about tomorrow. She doesn't notice acne, glasses, weight, mismatched clothing, or smudged mascara.

Skye laughs when my son burps, when someone drops an object, or when she hears a silly voice on the radio. She focuses on what is directly placed in front of her. When she wants to be alone, she tells everyone to "go away." When someone gets too close or makes her do something she doesn't like, she pushes and pinches and protests.

I wish I could push people away sometimes. I wish I could stop worrying about tomorrow. I wish I didn't judge others for their appearance and ·choices. I wish I just focused on each moment of time, savoring and maximizing every day.

I feel grateful for having the opportunity to raise Skye. I swell with pride when she breaks barriers, exhibits complicated thinking, or says a spontaneous word. Her NICU doctors would be astounded.

Although monotonous at times, I take care of my toddler-like child every day. I put on her shirt, shoes, and pants. I prepare her meals and cut up her food into small bites. I change her diaper and wash urine-soaked sheets. I fold up her special needs stroller and adjust the strapping when she grows taller. I buy weird toys that I know she will like. I brush her teeth and wash her face. I prepare her medications and bribe her with books and songs so she swallows them. I adjust her cumbersome orthopedic braces and splints.

For years, I've faced immense challenges. Perhaps some people wouldn't deal with it as well as I do. Perhaps others would deal with it better. I never had a choice. It is indeed the prophecy alluded to in "Welcome to Holland." A new normal exists for me and it's not so bad.

Fun Fact: Adam and I joke about a new disease called Skye Basch Syndrome.

Since she has so many random, complex symptoms, doctors add diagnoses all the time. Together, they make an impressive medical history. As of today, she has been formally diagnosed with: Hemiplegic Cerebral Palsy, Cortical Visual Impairment, Nystagmus, Optic Nerve Dysplasia, Epilepsy, Apraxia, Severe Speech Delay, Auditory Processing Disorder, Sensory Processing Disorder, Clawtoe, Hemifacial Spasms, and Trigeminal Neuralgia (probable). I'm probably forgetting a few.

I don't regret having children. I feel like Spiderman, who unexpectedly took on great power. My spider bite was giving birth to Skye. Sometimes I want to crawl into a hole and pretend I'm just a normal person.

But, while not a true superhero, I do have a responsibility to take care of my daughter. I also have a responsibility to take care of my son. I chose to have children. And I love them ferociously.

Being an advocate for Skye, I read articles and blogs, join listservs, and talk to other parents. I attend conferences and workshops and talk about essential oils, magnesium, chiropractors, adaptive bicycles, and spasticity.

My family and I have attended a pediatric epilepsy surgery conference every other summer. Many attendees had brain surgery for their epilepsy. Some had hemispherectomies like Skye. Some had lobe removal or partial lobe removal. Some had a series of escalating surgeries.

These former patients and their family members gather together in rotating national cities every other year. Top neurosurgeons, neurologists, physicians, nurses, lawyers, advocates, speech therapists, and school directors present valuable information about our kids.

Past talks included a lawyer advising how to set up a special needs trust, a school advocate explaining the IEP process, neurologists explaining post-surgery headaches, and an educational psychologist explaining how these children learn best.

My favorite part of the conference is that we spend a weekend with other people who get it. All the patients are missing key parts of their brains. Many are missing an entire hemisphere. All of us parents are way past hello. I have more in common with the other parents than I do with some of my closest friends.

Once I told a dad whose baby had just entered the NICU that I had been there for nine weeks. Jaw agape, disbelief spreading over his face, he stumbled for words or reaction. It's the same look I get when I tell people about my daughter's surgery.

Sometimes I don't want to tell people about the surgery because it just seems too crazy, too radical. If I'm not in the mood to explain my daughter's condition, I don't mention it. Because if you mention hemispherectomy, then you have to explain the reason that you chose to do it in the first place. People don't understand why a sane person would ever choose to disconnect an entire hemisphere. It's bizarre.

Skye has experienced more pain and suffering than most adults. She's endured a dozen surgeries, casts on every limb, toxic medications, needles, harsh nurses, hospital food, doctor appointments in every part of the state, years of physical therapy, and rigid limbs and joints.

I don't have it as bad as some people do and it's pointless to play the mind game of "who has it worse?" Nobody wins that game.

But, I wish every parent with typical children had Skye for one week. After watching her laugh and squeal and sing and face each day with determination and a wicked sense of humor, anyone would walk away with a new perspective.

Most people *believe* that their children are special. That may be true. But I *know* that mine is. So, thanks for following us along on the first part of her journey. We made it this far; now we just have to see if half a brain is enough to get Skye through high school and beyond.

Afterword

One day I attended a workshop on decreasing behavioral issues in children. One of the attendees told me that my child makes everyone else in the room feel better about theirs. I wanted to kick her in the shins. She laughed, indicating her comment's benign intention. I still felt humiliated and ashamed. Her child is so high functioning (cue vomiting noises) that she shouldn't have the license to call herself a parent of a child with special needs.

Based on this and other weird, rude, crazy, insulting, and zany interactions I've had since Skye's birth, it sounds like some of you may not know how to behave around parents who have children with special needs. Let's see if you've been paying attention.

Special Needs Quiz

1. You see a child with her mom at the public swimming pool. The child has obvious special needs. She reminds you (a little) of your cousin who has ADHD. You practice craniotomy voodoo, a technique you invented which may or may work. Do you:

    a.   Walk up to the mom and tell her she must try craniotomy voodoo immediately.

b. Walk up to the mom, ignore the daughter, and talk loudly about your cousin.
c. Walk up to the mom and hand her a cocktail. Smile at the daughter. Keep walking.

2. Your good friend just had a baby with special needs. Your friend seems frazzled and overwhelmed. You aren't very comfortable or familiar with any type of disability. When you see her child, you feel stressed and scared. Do you:
a. Stop calling your friend and wear disguises when you walk in front of her house.
b. Fake an illness, write a phony article about a cure in Peru, and then move there.
c. Grab some rags, mop, and Simple Green. Clean her house. Even the toilets.

3. You and some friends are talking about future plans. You mention that your son will probably go to Harvard and your daughter to Yale. Then you feel a little guilty. Your friend's kid has an intellectual disability so he will obviously never leave home and your miserable friend will be stuck with him forever. Do you:
a. Ask your friend if she wants to visit your children in Boston (if she can get away).
b. Ask your friend how it feels to know her life is ruined forever.
c. Ask your friend about her future plans. And her son's plans. They might surprise you.

Congratulations. You passed. No matter what situation presents itself, you've got this! Keep it simple. Open the door for someone struggling. Let a frazzled parent in front of you in line. Be comfortable with a little discomfort. If all else fails, just smile.

About the Author

Jenni Basch is an author, therapist, and special needs mama. She lives with her two children and husband in California. If she's not feeding her cats or reading about strong women, she might be enjoying a tasty beverage with friends.

For current promotions and information about upcoming books, sign up for the latest news here:

Author Page: jennibasch.com

Made in the USA
Coppell, TX
11 January 2021

47999579R00135